Towards a methodology for comparative quality assessment in European higher education

A pilot study on economics in Germany, the Netherlands and the United Kingdom

John Brennan
Leo C J Goedegebuure
Tarla Shah
Don F Westerheijden
Peter J M Weusthof

    June 1992

    ISBN 1 85824 000 X

Contents

Preface

This report is the result of a two-year exercise in international research co-operation. An international group of researchers from the CNAA (Council for National Academic Awards, London), HIS (Hochschul-Informations-System, Hanover) and CHEPS (Center for Higher Education Policy Studies, University of Twente) has been engaged in a pilot project to develop a valid, reliable and efficient method for comparisons of quality across higher education systems in several European countries.

The Dutch part of this pilot study is sponsored by the Ministry of Education and Science of the Netherlands. The project was supervised by a committee consisting of Dr P M M van Oijen and Drs C M M Paardekooper from the Ministry of Education and Science, Dr ir J P Th Kalkwijk from the Inspectorate for Higher Education, Dr ir K Kouwenaar from NUFFIC and Prof dr R A de Moor and Drs A I Vroeijenstijn from the Association of Universities (VSNU).

The authors wish to thank the members of this committee and all those who helped make the project a success. Particularly we should like to mention the 10 institutions (universities and polytechnics) and the 19 individual economists who were willing to co-operate in the collection of data about the 10 study programmes and, later, in the peer review meeting. The VSNU kindly helped in contacting the peers. We also wish to mention here our colleagues from HIS in Hanover, especially Edgar Frackmann and Michael Leszczensky, for providing invaluable information about German higher education. Our colleagues Frans van Vught at CHEPS and Richard Lewis at CNAA also made a major contribution to the design and overseeing of the project. A special word of thanks is due to the two staff members from CNAA, Josephine Falk and Nigel Nixon, who expertly assisted in drawing up the peer report during and after the meeting in Utrecht. Indispensable was, of course, the support we received from Agnes Nieuwenhuis, the secretary of CHEPS.

John Brennan
Leo Goedegebuure
Tarla Shah
Don Westerheijden
Peter Weusthof

1 Introduction

1.1 Quality in higher education within a European context

At present there is continued debate about the viability and effects of the anticipated European integration. Despite the multitude of political problems associated with a 'unified Europe', a strong belief exists that integration will be effectuated. In the field of higher education this has resulted in the widely held assumption that higher education institutions will be operating increasingly in a European framework, producing citizens living and working in an environment with few remaining national barriers. In this respect, the growth of a European labour market and the demand for a skilled work-force will extend employers' search for new graduates across different national systems of higher education. Similarly, the aspiration of students to study abroad and the enhanced opportunities for them to do so will lead to an increase of student mobility across national boundaries: as well as choosing between subjects and institutions, students will be choosing between different systems of higher education. Such trends reinforce each other and raise questions about the eventual emergence of a *European* higher education system.

National governments have a number of concerns in these matters. Economic competitiveness in the single market will be significantly influenced by the amount and quality of the skilled labour available to national economies. The returns on investment in higher education will also be viewed in an international context. If it takes longer and if it is more expensive to produce a graduate engineer in one country than another, are there any compensating advantages occurring from the additional investment? And, if students prefer to study abroad, for whatever reason, one might predict that increasing numbers will not return home; some countries, therefore, might be faced with a net outflow of skilled labour — a phenomenon already perfectly common on a regional basis in many nation states.

Many higher education institutions are developing substantial international activities: in research, student exchanges, joint study programmes, etc. For the individual higher education institution, Europe provides an extended arena — or, in keeping with the times, a market-place — in which it must compete for acceptance, prestige, students, staff and funding as it must in its local, regional and national arenas.

But it is not just a matter of competition. The academic enterprise is intrinsically co-operative and collegial. The standards of work of the individual academic, department or institution are referenced against the standards of work achieved elsewhere, both within countries and internationally. Thus, if institutions, departments and individual academics wish to assure their standards — which includes seeking ways of improving them — they will increasingly find a need for comparators from beyond their own countries.

7

All of the interested parties — governments, institutions, students and employers — are facing these issues within national higher education systems that are themselves expanding and diversifying. New kinds of institutions abound, with fresh and frequently changing names. New distinctive non-university sectors are emerging in some countries just as older non-university sectors are poised to disappear into enlarged unitary systems in others. The same can be said of qualifications and study programmes.

It is this rapidly changing European higher education scene that provides the context for the present study being undertaken jointly by the Center for Higher Education Policy Studies (CHEPS) in the Netherlands, the Council for National Academic Awards (CNAA) in the United Kingdom, and the Hochschul-Informations-System (HIS) in Germany. The impetus for the project came from the Dutch government arising out of a concern about the quality of graduates being produced by Dutch higher education within the European context.

1.1.1 The comparative quality issue in Dutch higher education

In November 1988 the then Dutch Minister of Education and Science, W Deetman, asked the Advisory Council on Higher Education (ARHO) to advise on the adaptation of the Dutch higher education system to 'Europe 1992'. The central question posed by the Minister was whether Dutch higher education was suitably prepared for the international competition arising out of the integrated European market. The ARHO published its advice 13 months later.[1] The Council was worried. It doubted the extent to which the Netherlands could provide high quality education, top quality research and could use the opportunities arising out of the ongoing process of European unification. The Council concluded, from discussions with experts, that the image of university graduates abroad was not unqualifiedly positive. It listed four possible reasons for this perception:[2]

- a lack of quality with respect to the object of comparison;
- the formal characteristics of the Dutch higher education system, which lead to an incorrect image of education, especially because of the combination of short formal length of studies, uniformity of this in the university and non-university sector, and admission rights for graduates from both sectors to PhD programmes;
- unfamiliarity with the level and content of Dutch higher education;
- lack of interest or protectionism in several countries.

NUFFIC, the Dutch organisation for international co-operation in higher education, has also expressed anxieties about the valuation of Dutch higher education diplomas in other countries.* According to NUFFIC, the problem is more a question of under-valuation than of bad quality, for which it provides three reasons:[3]

- doubts in the Netherlands about the academic quality of the newly introduced Two Tier Structure in university education, which may indeed be a source of concern compared to earlier Dutch university education, but is unnecessary when compared to higher education levels in other countries;

---

* EC countries, the USA, Australia and Third World countries were included in this study.

8

- bad marketing: the structure and quality of Dutch higher education are too little known outside the Netherlands;
- lack of interest: in other countries more characteristics are demanded than Dutch higher education provides, or there is politically induced protectionism.

On the other hand, the present Minister of Education and Science, J Ritzen, in his reaction to the ARHO advice, stated in Parliament that the situation was not that bad. He argued that there exists, indeed, an opinion that Dutch higher education is doing a good job despite various criticisms. The more positive perceptions on the quality of Dutch higher education received authoritative support when, in April 1990, the OECD published its *Review of Educational Policy in the Netherlands*. The examiners:[4]

> *emerged, in fact, with the conviction that the Dutch are perhaps too critical of their own educational system which has, by most measures of short and long term productivity, been largely successful.*

This is not to say that the OECD examiners found nothing to criticise in Dutch higher education, for the report's summative conclusion is that although Dutch education (including higher education) reaches a good quality level, it is expensive.

To sum up: the situation is far from clear. Conflicting statements are made about the quality of Dutch higher education, about the *perceived* quality of Dutch diplomas, and about the guessed-at causes of this situation. In most of the cases mentioned above it is not known in what way judgements about Dutch higher education are established (which information is gathered and how, what are the criteria and norms, and so on). In the reports of both the ARHO and NUFFIC it is stated that there is a lack of data on higher education systems that is suitable for international comparison. This reinforces the opinion that rather far-reaching conclusions are drawn by various interested parties based on sketchy and partial information. Again, truth appears to be in the eye of the beholder.

1.1.2 The comparative quality issue in German higher education

With not much more than appropriate exaggeration it can be said that the comparative quality issue does not exist in higher education in Germany* — quality as such was, until recently, not an issue. Rather, the issues in the debate about higher education in Germany concerned the length of time students need to obtain their degree and questions surrounding the status of *Fachhochschulen* and *Gesamthochschulen*.[5] More recently, the growing number of student that have to be accommodated in a situation of constant budget appropriations, has made the student view of quality of 'delivery' and context of the teaching process into another issue.[6] Formal systems of quality assessment, comparable to the institutional arrangements in either the Netherlands or the United Kingdom, do not exist in Germany, neither at the national nor at the *Länder* level. The quality of higher education is generally *trusted* to be high, because of the high entry qualifications pertaining both to students and to staff appointments.[7] As a consequence of this situation, the present project had to begin practically from scratch in Germany.

---

* It should be noted that the description is based on the situation in the *Länder* that were part of the *Bundesrepublik* before October 1990.

1.1.3 Quality issues in higher education in the United Kingdom

During the course of the project the British government published proposals for a fundamental re-organisation of higher education, to include the dismantling of the long-standing binary divide between universities and polytechnics. The proposals included the linkage of quality assessment to the funding of institutions and the introduction of new system-wide arrangements for quality assurance of and within institutions. These arrangements also entailed the closure of the Council for National Academic Awards (CNAA), the UK sponsor of the project described in this report.

The CNAA's interest in the project arose partly in response to the growing concern by the funding councils and others to make comparisons of quality for purposes of funding allocation. The CNAA approach to threshold quality assurance and quality support and enhancement through peer review had deliberately avoided questions of comparative quality. Such questions were however now being placed firmly on the agenda and CNAA was concerned that valid and reliable methodologies be developed to provide answers to them.

However, the CNAA's prime concern was that of a national degree-awarding body responsible for the standards of its awards. Throughout its 25 year history, CNAA had sought to ensure the national comparability of its awards, from whichever of its 100 plus institutions they had been achieved. With increasing numbers of students on Erasmus programmes or otherwise studying abroad and with the coming of the single market and 'Europeanisation' of the graduate labour market, CNAA's concerns about the comparability of standards were seen now to extend beyond the borders of the UK. Exploration of possible methods for the comparison of quality was seen as a necessary first step in addressing such issues.

It should be noted, however, that notwithstanding the CNAA's interest in the project, there was no widespread concern expressed about UK academic standards, either by government or by the general public, even though the expansion of higher education had for some time far outpaced the expansion of resources. The comparability of UK higher education and its graduates with those of other countries was not regarded as an issue.

1.2 Aim of the study, approach, and structure of the report

The Dutch Minister of Education and Science approached CHEPS to investigate whether a methodology could be developed from which sound and reliable comparisons of the quality of higher education in different countries could be made. The aim of the present study therefore is to assess the possibility of providing valid and reliable comparisons of the quality of higher education in several European countries. This has been operationalised in the following central research question:

Which instruments, procedures and additional means exist to make valid comparisons of the quality of higher education in different countries?

It should be stressed that the focus of the study is not on the comparison of quality as such. Rather, an attempt is made to identify possible ways to approach the substantial problems that are part and parcel of international comparative assessments. Neither rankings nor 'better or worse' statements are the objective. Primarily, the study should be seen as a methodological exercise undertaken to shed more light on the actual possibilities of making comparative statements with respect to national higher education systems. Because of the remarkably barren nature of this area of research, the present study is a pilot project. It is not assumed beforehand that a first attempt at devising a suitable methodology for international quality comparison at the system level will result in *the* definite method. The complexities associated with the issue of quality comparison would make such an objective more than brash. It is envisaged that the research project could be a starting point for an incremental process that, on the basis of the outcomes of this endeavour and others, evaluation and improvement, in the longer run may lead to a usable method of international quality comparison. A last qualification of this study is that it is focused solely on the teaching function of higher education. Notwithstanding the interconnectedness of teaching and research in the field of higher education, in order to limit the complexity of the project no attention is paid to research as an academic activity.

The structure of the report is as follows. In Chapter 2 a brief account of methods of quality comparison is presented. After discussing the ever problematic nature of the quality concept, we focus on the two best known methods of assessing quality: peer review and performance indicators. The pros and cons of both methods are presented, resulting in a choice for triangulation. Peer review informed by performance indicator type of data is perceived to be a viable option for the research under question. In Chapter 3 the design of the project is elaborated upon. After explaining the rationale for the use of an open systems approach and the choice of a particular discipline (economics) as the empirical focus of the study, the logic of a two-stage approach for the comparative method is outlined. In stage one, information is gathered based on a checklist resulting from the open systems perspective. The outcomes of the data collection are presented in separate publications (for the contents of which, see Appendix II), while in Chapter 4 the method and process of the data collection is presented. This information will be used as the input for stage two in which, as an experiment, an international committee of peers has attempted to form an assessment of the quality of economics from a comparative perspective. In Chapter 5 the design, process and outcomes of the international peer review are reported. Although the method has proven to be successful to some extent, there also appear to be major problems associated with it. These are discussed in the final chapter, in which the attempt to develop a suitable method for international quality comparisons is evaluated, with particular reference to the essential component of the peer review process. Several suggestions for improvement are made to overcome some of the problems likely to be encountered in subsequent projects of this kind.

2 On methods of quality comparison

2.1 The concept of quality

We shall not go into the discussion of what *essentially* is quality. A single, substantive definition of it is not possible — the one figure who almost found one, the Phaedrus in Pirsig's novel, went crazy when he found it, so all we are left with is the famous quotation: 'But when you try to say what the quality is, apart from the things that have it, it all goes *poof!* There's nothing to talk about.' [8] Against the view that definitions are important, which he calls *essentialism*, Popper has argued vehemently and convincingly:

> *essentialism is mistaken in suggesting that definitions can add to our* knowledge of facts *(although* qua *decisions about conventions they may be influenced by our knowledge of facts, and although they create instruments which may in their turn influence the formation of our theories and thereby the evolution of our knowledge of facts).* [9]

More viable from an epistemological point of view (and more mentally sane from Phaedros' point of view) is the notion that quality is 'fitness for purpose' [10] and that it depends on the subject's view on the purposes of higher education to say what is quality. Thus there are (at least) as many definitions of quality in higher education as there are categories of stakeholders (such as students, teaching staff, scientific communities, government and employers), *times* the number of purposes, or dimensions, these stakeholders distinguish.

This does not tell us what to look for when we are interested in observing quality of higher education, but it does provide the necessary sensitivity to the fact that quality can be viewed from different perspectives and that each perspective consists of multiple dimensions.

2.1.1 Quality of what?

In keeping with the (broadly seen) two possible answers to the question of what it is that higher education is 'producing', two objects for the assessment of quality present themselves. On the one hand, one can concentrate on the quality of the *output*, the graduates. What is their quality on the labour market, or, viewed in a broader context, what is their gain in terms of personal qualities from experiencing higher education? On the other hand, one can argue that higher education is providing education, a study programme, to students, and that it is the quality of this *process* that is to be assessed.

Given the background of the project, we are eventually interested in the graduate's quality. As the study programme and its immediate context (forms of teaching, staff–student ratio, physical environment, remedial teaching programmes, etc) are the factors that can be manipulated by those engaged in higher education, we focus on the *process*. This is the choice commonly made

— though usually less explicit — in quality assessment; a more direct, workable, approach to quality of graduates apparently has not yet been found. In doing so, we of course realise that other factors besides these 'process variables' determine the quality of a certain graduate. The student's personality, prior educational experience, intellectual capacity, etc, are clear examples in this respect. However, as they cannot be directly influenced by higher education, these fall within the realm of the context variables (see Chapter 3).

This still does not tell us exactly what or how will be observed. As the *how* to a large extent influences the *what*, we first address the 'how' question. From this, a list of variables to be included in the research will be developed.

2.1.2 Threshold quality or relative quality

The way accreditation agencies usually judge educational programmes involves the decision whether the programme satisfies a number of criteria. Usually these criteria are centrally (eg nationally) decided upon, but they may also be criteria implied by the goals set for the specific study programme. If these are met, the programme has 'passed the test', it is acknowledged as a genuine higher education level study programme. This way of looking at quality requires a (preferably explicit) set of criteria against which the programme is to be judged. Furthermore, the only interesting question is 'pass or fail?' — not whether the programme passes by a narrow or a wide margin, or whether it has improved, for instance, since the previous assessment.

Another way of looking at quality does not require previous definition of a set of (absolute) criteria, but is concerned with relative quality. *Relative quality* is the concept that immediately comes to mind when either diachronous comparisons have to be made of a single study programme (such as whether it has improved since the previous assessment, or when synchronous comparisons are made ie comparisons between study programmes in different institutions.

2.2 Methods for assessment of quality in higher education

There are two basic methods of assessing quality of education. One is based on performance indicators and other inter-subjective data, the other on evaluations by experts ('peer review'). When speaking of *performance indicators* one is tempted to think in the first place of quantitative measures. Qualitative performance indicators exist too, however. An authoritative definition of performance indicators does not exist. Many aspects and categories of performance indicators can be distinguished,[11] but for the present purpose it is enough to differentiate between performance indicators and peer review, so a relatively simple definition will suffice: performance indicators are empirical, quantitative or qualitative data that point to a system's (either conceived as nation or institution) goal achievement.[12] When the concept of indicators is used in this study, it is in this broad sense — not in the narrow, 'reductionist' sense of quantitative, preferably financial, data.

The traditional example of *peer review* is the referee system of scientific journals. An anonymous output of scientific activity (a manuscript) is judged by a few anonymous fellow scientists (peers) who are reputed to possess sufficient expertise on the questions addressed in the article. The norms and criteria they use in their judgement are the canons of the methods

14

and subject matters of 'good science' that dominate the particular discipline. These norms are not, as a rule, fully explicit; it is impossible to define *a priori* the characteristics that make an article 'superb', whether it concerns the 'craftsmanship' and literary value expected from a historian, or the parsimoniousness and elegance of a mathematical treatise.[13] Even less are such norms inter-subjective.* Another example of peer review is provided by the study by the Advisory Council for Research Policy (RAWB) on health science in the Netherlands: here, among other methods, a sample of scientists from the international field were asked in a questionnaire to judge different aspects of the Dutch peers' research.[14] Again, the norms used by the respondents remained unknown. It is this — as far as we know inevitable — subjectivity that forms the distinguishing characteristic of peer review.

In the context of quality assessment in higher education the concept of peer review is often used somewhat loosely. All methods where human judgement is involved are then called peer review. The judgements may or may not be informed by more or less objective databases (among them performance indicators), the judges may or may not be peers. What are peers is not clear either. Peer review as it is known in science studies involves scientists from the discipline under consideration who have a high reputation in their field. Sometimes it is maintained, however, that peers should not differ too much in reputation from the persons whose quality they are to assess. This makes the circle of peers that can act as assessors in each particular case much smaller and also makes it very difficult to produce a discipline-wide assessment, given the existence within a discipline of research groups with highly different reputations. The definition of peers is sometimes broadened, on the other hand, to include not just scientists, but also representatives of 'audiences' for the discipline under investigation, such as members of industry, employers and professionals. The latter, broad, definition is the one often used in practice. The choice between peer review and performance indicators is partly a function of the objectives of the assessment. When the objectives call for precision and simplicity — eg when funding is a stake — the numerical scores produced by performance indicators may be required. When the objectives concern improvement or enhancement of quality, the nuances and complexity of peer judgement may be preferred.

2.2.1 Performance indicators in practice

Many performance indicators, notably those of research, are based on peer review procedures. For example, only when the peer referee process of a top journal has been successfully completed can a researcher 'score' on the publication counting performance indicators. Citation performance indicators develop this theme some steps further, because for citations to occur not only does a publication have to be made, but other researchers (peers) have to judge the publication worth citing and their own publications must appear in (refereed) top journals (other journals are not covered by the (*Social*) *Science Citation Index*, which is often the basis for citation scores). Another example, also based on peer judgements of quality, is the success in obtaining grants from (inter)national research agencies.

There are fewer performance indicators for the quality of teaching and higher education courses.[15] If any performance indicators are suggested for education, they are proxies that are

---

* Inter-subjectivity means that a phenomenon will appear the same to any observer; in the case of indicators each observer will 'read' the same 'value' from a given instrument or indicator.

often further removed from the concept they intend to gauge than the peer review based performance indicators for research. Most performance indicators for teaching used in practice are concerned with efficiency (such as staff–student ratios, costs per student) or effectiveness (eg number or proportion of graduations, (un-)employment figures).[16] The difficulty of the subject has raised questions on the viability of the use of performance indicators for the teaching function.[17]

The greatest advantage of performance indicators is their inter-subjectivity. This offers a possibility to compare institutions, disciplines, etc. And it provides a relatively firm base for decision-making when compared to the subjectivity of peer review procedures.

Disadvantages of performance indicators are known too. First there is the question of relevance.[18] 'Standards of quality have focused on those aspects that are easiest to count. But these measures do not reveal what colleges and universities actually do.'[19] Performance indicators are partial operationalisations of quality that do not cover all dimensions of the concept; they produce a distorted picture. Or objective data exist only for phenomena that are hard to connect to quality, as is true for education. Second, there are practical problems. Databases are not very reliable, or cannot be compared. This problem arises even when comparing institutions within a country; in international comparative research this factor again is magnified substantially. Third, performance indicators invite behaviour that 'scores', instead of behaviour geared to higher quality[20] — unless the performance indicator necessarily correlates perfectly with the quality concept it intends to measure, which, as performance indicators are partial measures, is an utopian ideal. Finally, as performance indicators of research in large proportion are based on peer review, their objectivity can be disputed, and comparisons across entities then become precarious. Such problems, reducing the content validity of indicators, are always present when designing objective measurement.

2.2.2 The practice of peer review

The assessment processes existing of old in the various disciplines were peer review processes geared to 'intrinsic' research goals, ie scientific quality and progress only. The new evaluation processes, however, not only cover both research and teaching — though not necessarily within one procedure — they are also geared to other, 'extrinsic' goals, such as social relevance and accountability towards the funding organisations.

The advantage of peer review lies in its high content validity. It is the only way to assess quality directly, without proxy indicators. Moreover, peer review is a flexible method that can be adjusted to traditions in all disciplines (or lower entities such as paradigmatic schools: in paradigmatically fragmented disciplines one can only give judgements within schools, since reputations are only valid within the field of adherents to a certain paradigm).

The most important disadvantage of peer review is its subjectivity. The judgements always result from, in principle, unverifiable mental processes in the judges. The basis of the peer review process therefore remains something of a black Box. Group judgements and explicit argumentation of the judgements are only a partial remedy to this, as they may be influnced by social processes. Sociological research into the actual operation of the traditional peer review processes has discovered another, associated, disadvantage: even in the old days other factors than scientific quality influenced the judgements of peers. Educational, social and institutional backgrounds of reviewer and reviewed played an important role,[21] and random fluctuations were not to be ignored.[22] Despite its high content validity, the reliability of peer review is, therefore, low.

2.2.3 The best of both worlds: peer review informed by performance indicators

In line with the methodological advice that when several imperfect measurement strategies are available, it is good practice to 'triangulate' results of one method by those of another, the practice has developed to use performance indicators not on face value, but to use them 'intelligently'.* This means the data are put in the hands of a committee of peers who can, from their expertise, evaluate the data and who can supplement them with their knowledge of the field. On the other hand, objective indicators put reins on the otherwise uncontrolled subjective judgements of peer reviewers.

It is hoped that this mixed method provides 'the best of both worlds', though there is no way to know this. (If there were a method that could be used as a criterion for this, we should use this method and not the less perfect approximations!) We will come back to this point in the final chapter. The design of the present study is based on this logic: a trial peer review will be preceded by the collection of quantitative and qualitative, inter-subjective, indicator-type data. This will be elaborated on in the next chapter.

---

* See also the data on the emerging patterns in British and Dutch quality assessment systems in higher education, as evidenced in, eg Goedegebuure, Maassen & Westerheijden (eds.), 1990.

3 Design of the project

3.1 The complexity of international comparison

It is evident — from what has been said so far — that observing quality of higher education is never an easy matter. Also, there are vast methodological difficulties in defining quality in higher education. These problems are, however, multiplied when comparing quality internationally. A brief overview can suffice to highlight some major complications.

First, the various elements of higher education systems have different characteristics in different countries: the input differs in that staff–student ratios vary widely; the relationships with the environment differ, because, eg funding levels by governments differ; institutions differ, in the sense that what in one country is within the exclusive realm of university teaching, can be taught in another country in other kinds of institutions as well; the educational processes differ in that they take three years in one country, and four or five in others; the goals of these processes differ, from specialised training in one country to general education in another.

Second, categories of stakeholders, and the power balances among them, differ in different countries, with consequent variations in the socially accepted definition of the quality of higher education. Moreover, distinct dimensions of quality may be emphasised by categories of stakeholders in each country. For example, government policies may vary among countries, resulting in a different weighting of dimensions of the quality ('cheaply' educated labour force against broad individual development at top-level no matter what it costs in time and money).

Third, national traditions regarding the acceptability of methods of quality assessment differ: in one country performance indicators are accepted and used regularly, while in another they are treated with great suspicion; or peer review is not accepted in one country because of its corruptibility by cartels of colleagues, while in the other country it is perceived to be the only legitimate method.

Finally, it is already far from easy to reach national agreement on definitions of data to be used as performance indicators, or even just as statistics. But internationally, the chances are slight at best that such definitions are the same even in only two countries. This problem is aggravated (or perhaps caused) by the fact that concepts or phenomena that on the surface seem to be the same in different countries, on closer inspection appear to have different meanings, because of the differences in the context in which they are used. This often is a consequence of the multifarious structures of the higher education systems. It means that data (whether quantitative or qualitative), even if present for all programmes within a national higher education system, will hardly ever be comparable internationally.

19

Still, some aspects of higher education in the different countries remain that are more or less the same. One important example is that higher education always strives to pass on the best of a discipline's knowledge to a new generation of students. Some commonality is an absolute requirement, without which comparison of higher education internationally would become impossible. But given this common core, the challenge is to find a way of mapping the different qualities of the various national higher education systems, recognising their unique strengths and weaknesses.

3.2 Delimitation of the scope

Assessment of quality in higher education is a complex question, and an international comparison of it is even more complex, but this does not imply that it is not possible at all. However, to keep such a comparison manageable, a rigorous delimitation of its scope is necessary.

Keeping in mind that education is always education *in* something, we shall not try to focus on *the* quality of higher education, but approach the quality of educational characteristics *in a certain discipline* as the empirical testing ground for the comparative method to be developed. An appropriate discipline for a pilot project should have an internationally recognisable body of common knowledge: several subjects, or methods, etc, that are part of the knowledge every peer in the disciplinary community should possess. This requirement rules out some of the 'soft' disciplines of the humanities and social sciences. On the other hand, for a pilot study it is interesting to study a discipline where some national differences may exist, not only in the environment of the educational programme (eg government policy, student age at entry, number of years of study), but also in the educational process itself. For while it may be interesting in its own right to observe the influence of environmental factors on an otherwise identical study programme, for a pilot project it is advisable to check every part of the analytical scheme. This makes some of the 'hard' disciplines, such as physics or chemistry, less attractive. Supposedly, in those sciences the disciplinary 'core' is so large and the content of study programmes is so much controlled by the international disciplinary community, that national differences are relatively unimportant. Almost the same argument can be propounded when considering the labour market for graduates from the different disciplines. As a 'golden middle' in between the two extremes, *economics* has been chosen as the discipline for this pilot study. Economics has a common body of knowledge, consisting of micro-economic theory (theory of individual choice, utility maximisation principle), macro-economic approaches (neo-classical, Keynesian, and post-Keynesian economics) and a common language (economic-mathematical modelling). However, this leaves enough room for national differentiation, eg, in the extent to which institutional economics, economical law, or econometrics are part of what is expected from graduates at the national level. Viewing the labour market, an internationally recognisable 'economist' exists, as do country-specific profiles.

Given the expected importance of national, system-wide characteristics, and the complexity of any one higher education system, the number of countries to be involved in the project had to be limited. The participating countries in the project are the Federal Republic of Germany, the Netherlands and the United Kingdom. In practice, the overview of Germany has been limited to the *Bundesländer* that were part of the federal republic at the start of the project, in 1989; for the United Kingdom, attention has been focused on England.

Within these countries, different types of higher education exist, and different levels of academic degrees. Regarding degrees, it was decided to concentrate on the first, most common university degree, that is the *Diplom* (or equivalent) in Germany, the *doctorandus* in the Netherlands, and the *Bachelor's* in the United Kingdom. Consequently it was decided that from the continental systems, non-university types of institutions the - *Fachhochschulen* and *Hogescholen* (*HBO-institutions*) - would not be taken into account, as they award different degrees. On the British side, however, *polytechnics* were included in the project, since both universities and polytechnics award *Bachelor's* degrees.

It will be noted that this selection of degrees differs from existing practice within European countries in the various 'equivalence of degree' programmes. In those, there is great pressure to equate the Dutch and German university degree with the second British degree, the Master's degree. In general, continental countries consider a Bachelor's degree an incomplete university programme.[23] In this study the choice has been made for an initial comparison of the Bachelor programme with programmes that lead to a *Diplom* or *Doctorandus* degree. The *a priori* assumption that the nominal study length is the indication for the quality of graduates has not been made. This is but one of the empirical questions to be addressed in the project. We therefore decided to focus on the first degree that students in the three countries can obtain after completion of their secondary education and which serves as the terminal qualification with which most graduates enter the labour market. We consider this to be a more justified approach in trying to get a valid and reliable judgement of the quality aspects of higher education from an international perspective. Moreover, the Bachelor's degree is accepted in the United Kingdom as a full degree, in the sense that it is considered a final qualification, recognised by the labour market. Also, most students do take a Bachelor's degree, while only a small minority goes on for a Master's.

3.3 A systems theoretical approach to higher education

For the purpose of this study, higher education has been observed from a systems theoretical point of view. The reason for choosing this approach is because it provides us with generally applicable concepts that are consistently useful in both developing the methodology for comparison and the subsequent empirical analysis. *Systems* consist of interrelated elements.[24] This means that the state of any *element* is determined by the states of the other elements within the system. The boundary of a system is, in principle, defined by the boundary of relations (systems are 'closed'); in practice a more arbitrary decision is made to ignore less important or less frequent relations. Or the researcher focuses on a system that is viewed as an element of a larger *super-system*, with which it has important relations (open system approach). Individuals or units (actors) may be acting according to the theory or 'principle of action' the researcher postulates for the system. Actors may be found on different levels of the system; the lowest level the researcher wishes to study is called the 'atomic' or *'individual'* actor (both 'atomic' and 'individual' mean 'indivisible'), but higher levels of organised individuals can be discerned as well, which may be organised in even higher-level organisations themselves (layers of sub-systems, for example: individual scientists → research groups → faculties → institutions → intermediate organisations). It is the researcher who decides which level is most appropriate for a certain study.

21

For this pilot study, we do not have to choose a 'principle of action', because we are only interested in the statics of existing relations among the elements and the dimensions along which the system can be described, not in the dynamics of action in the system (how one element influences the state of others). All that needs to be said about the action is that, in the systems approach, it is usual to view it as a *process* among or within the elements. Other elements that do not act on their own accord, but provide the conditions under which the actors operate are called the (internal) *environment* of the actors. The external environment is made up of the elements of the super-system of which the system under investigation is also an element.

Processes exist of *input*, *throughput* (or the *process* in the strict sense), and *output* (plus, if necessary, the *feedback* of output via the environment of the actor to the input of a new round of the process). These concepts were used to describe, analyse and understand higher education in the three countries included in the study.

Viewing higher education as a system that contains environment, input, process and output elements, leads us to the question of which system level is to be the focus for comparison. The original intention of the project was to concentrate on the national level: in what ways are the qualities of economics programmes different from each other in the three countries? The basic idea behind this was that system-wide characteristics are the boundary conditions for any higher education programme within that country. For example, the nominal number of years of study is often determined nationally, as is the certification of study programmes or the entry qualifications.

It was clear from the outset, however, that there is not just *between-country variance*, but also *within-country variance*. In every academic discipline, some sort of status-hierarchy exists for the individual peers. This results in a status-hierarchy of institutions (which partly leads its own life; if, for instance, a highly respected professor moves from one institution to another, this does not automatically result in a proportional reduction of status for the institution). In European higher education, this institutional hierarchy is often informal; there are no Carnegie classifications or authoritative rankings on this side of the Atlantic.[25] Furthermore, in many European countries, the basic equality of all institutions (within a given sector of higher education) is a premise of higher education policy. Still, (informal) hierarchies do exist, as evidenced by the 'Oxbridge complex' in the United Kingdom, or by the rumour-like knowledge peers all have of their own discipline. To take this within-country variance seriously, the level of the individual study programme has been chosen as the focus of comparison.

Recognition of the differences among individual study programmes does not imply a neglect of the influence of higher-level factors that might influence the quality of higher education. Moreover, the relative importance of the different levels is not known beforehand. Therefore, a multi-level approach has been chosen in this project, although the emphasis is on the study programmes (see also Figure 1). Consequently, decisions also had to be made about the study programmes to be involved, since it would not be feasible to cover all economics programmes in the three countries. Ten economics study programmes have been selected as broadly typical examples in the countries concerned. In the British case, they are from two universities and two polytechnics, the latter included because of the size and equivalence of standards of the British polytechnic sector. In Germany as well as in the Netherlands the economics study programmes in three economic faculties of universities were analysed.

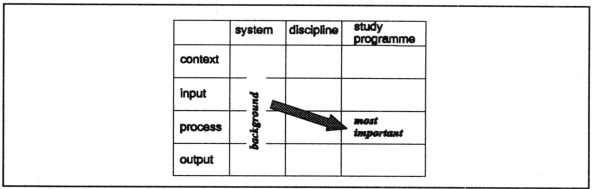

Figure 1 Scheme of Multi-Level Approach of Project

3.4 Aims and research methods

The central research question as formulated in Chapter 1 can, from a Dutch point of view, be translated in the following way: how does the quality of higher education in the Netherlands relate to the quality of higher education in other European countries?

To obtain an answer to this question, a methodology was developed jointly by the participants in this project, the CNAA, HIS and CHEPS. This methodology consists of two stages:

- collection and analysis of descriptive information about systems and study programmes;
- international peer review of selected study programmes.

The objective of the first stage was to gather relevant information about the three higher education systems for an international peer review on which the peers could base their judgements regarding the 10 programmes under study. Before the data collection was started a checklist was developed. By this list the data were collected. The scheme of the checklist corresponds to the aggregation levels (national system, discipline and study programme) and system features (input, environment, process and output) mentioned in Figure 1. These concepts were also used to describe, analyse and understand the higher education systems in the three countries. This information was the 'input' for the second phase: the international peer review. The data was collected during the period January to May 1991. The first phase will be elaborated on in Chapter 4.

The aim of the peer review was to come to a balanced judgement on the quality differences between comparable categories of graduates in Germany, the United Kingdom and the Netherlands, in the circumstances of the different structural characteristics of the higher education systems and education programmes. This second phase consisted of organising and executing an international peer review. The quantitative and qualitative data that were collected was used by economics experts, who formed an international peer committee. During a two-day meeting in Utrecht in July 1991 they discussed the documentation prepared in the first stage. The experts came from the three countries involved. The peer review will be elaborated on in Chapter 5.

4 The data collection process

4.1 Collection and presentation of written data

As indicated before, data had been collected based on a checklist developed out of the system perspective. The structure of this checklist was based on the system/process view of higher education as shown in Figure 1 (input, process and output) and the different system levels (system, discipline and study programme). On the basis of this checklist, which contains a large number of features, data were collected about the different higher education systems in the countries mentioned.

1 Checklist, systems level

Input features
- o age, educational, work and other experience of entering students;
- o methods of enrolment selection;
- o proportion of 18-24 year age group participation;
- o staff-student ratios;
- o academic staff expertise, qualifications and experience.

Process features
- o length of study programmes;
- o completion/transfer rates;
- o main forms of teaching and learning;
- o main forms of assessment;
- o forms of course organisation, particularly regarding student choice;
- o kinds of staff-student interaction.

Environmental features
- o structure of the system: types of institutions, funding arrangements, qualification structures, quality control mechanisms, government's (and/or other central agencies') 'steering philosophy';
- o overall resource levels, state of facilities generally;
- o staff development, career prospects, age profile, 'morale';
- o balance of teaching, research and other functions;
- o forms and modes of external control on academic programmes, work of individual academics;
- o facilities for students: financial, accommodation, etc;
- o forms of institutional governance and management.

The first level of the checklist is *the national system level* (Box 1). The information at this level is intended to provide the context for comparison of quality by clarifying what should be compared with what in the different systems. The system level is an important level, because the quality of education cannot be defined out of the context of the educational system. The following input, process and output features are included in the checklist.

The second level on which we looked for data was *the discipline level*. At this level we described elements common to all study programmes in economics in a country's higher education system. The following questions are important in this respect:

- in which sectors of the higher education system can this study programme be studied: university and/or non-university?
- what are, broadly speaking, the differences between the study programmes on both sides of the binary line (if it can be studied in both sectors)?
- which specialisms exist within the field?
- how many students (full-time and/or part-time) study this subject in each sector of higher education, compared to the total number of students in the sectors?
- what are, broadly speaking, the job prospects of graduates in this field - if necessary detailed for sectors or specialisms?

On the basis of these questions the following discipline dimensions were included in the checklist (see Box 2).

2 Checklist, discipline-wide level

> o in which sectors of higher education can this subject be studied?
> o are there differences in content or objectives between sectors?
> o what are the main specialisms?
> o how many students (full-time or part-time) study the subject in each sector, compared to the total number of students in the sectors?
> o what are, broadly speaking, the job prospects of graduates in this field — if necessary detailed for sectors of specialisms?
> o are there disciplinary links external to higher education (eg, professional groups)?
> o is the subject typically studied alongside other subjects and, if so, which?

At the lowest and most important level, the study programme level, we have collected information on three or four more or less typical study programmes per country. Here we were looking for information about study programmes that were offered in certain faculties. The information at this level consisted of, among others, a detailed description of the course structure, course units, organised into core subjects and specialisations, entry level and exit level examination questions in core subjects and in some important optional subjects. An overview of all the aspects can be found in Box 3.

In first instance the information needed was obtained from existing documents. The documents used were:

- policy documents (government documents, institutional documents and faculty documents);
- study guide-lines or study handbooks;

3 Checklist, programme level

Input dimensions
- presence or absence of admission requirements for potential students such as: entrance examination, the need for certain subjects or levels in secondary education;
- number of foreign languages that potential students are familiar with;
- staff-student ratios per study programme of location;
- academic staff qualifications: eg, proportion of PhDs;
- library and computer facilities;
- level of student demand (ratio of places to applications);
- type of students enroled, eg, gender, age, class background;
- total number of students in each cohort.

Process dimensions
- the study programme:
  - number of years of study;
  - content and level of courses;
  - sequence and other connections between courses;
  - interdisciplinary of disciplinary study programme;
  - flexibility of the study programme (freedom of choice of courses);
  - level of final examinations or final papers;
  - number of selection moments during the study;
  - forms of assessment;
- the way education is 'delivered' to the students:
  - type of educational interaction: student centred or teacher centred (lectures, lab courses, study projects, training in practice);
  - proportion of time devoted to lab and practice training;
  - the conditions under which this takes place: availability and quality of classrooms, of library and computer facilities;
- student counselling (eg, mentor or tutor);
- proportion of successful leavers (or, inversely, drop-out rate);
- factual as compared to nominal study length;
- study load (hours per year);
- uniform or pluriform study length.

Output dimensions
- initial destinations: employed, full-time education, unemployed;
- proportion of graduated working in scientific and non-scientific sector (six months after graduation);
- proportion of PhDs (10 years after graduation);
- extent to which graduates are recruited to specialist or general jobs;
- mean salary of graduates in first job (after six months) compared with average for all graduates;
- main types of employment;
- main types of employers.

- statistical overviews;
- self-study reports;
- research publications;
- existing descriptions of (higher) education systems;
- information brochures for students.

A more detailed overview of documents that were used can be found in the list of references. During the data collection it appeared that not all information that was needed was available in the documents. To fill these gaps we sent institutions a checklist in which they could write down the missing information. We also visited institutions to get complementary information. The decision was made to gather data which was as recent as possible (preferably 1989–1990 data, not older than 1986).

After finishing the data collection we composed five documents as the input for the international peer review (see Chapter 5). Volume I contains a concise description of the German, Dutch and British higher education systems within which the economics study programmes are located. The relevant information is structured along the components of the system model: environment, input, process and output. (Volume I has been published as a comparison volume to this report.)

On the same basis in Volume II information is provided about the discipline that was object of study: economics.

The documents IIa (Germany), IIb (The Netherlands) and IIc (United Kingdom) contain detailed information about the selected study programmes per country. This information is structured as follows:

- a comparative overview of the course structure;
- the content of the core courses: micro-economics and macro-economics;
- the courses offered under the quantitative methods theme;
- an overview of the specialist strands.

Besides these five documents, for each separate participating university an appendix was made. This contains additional information about the study programmes. For an overview of the contents, see Appendix II, section VI.

4.2 A preliminary assessment of the data collection process

Doing international research appeared to be a complicated matter. We had to deal with the sometimes very large differences between national higher education systems. For instance, the sharp distinction in the Netherlands and Germany between universities and polytechnics does not exist in this way in the United Kingdom. In the latter country one can obtain a Bachelor's and a Master's and a Doctorate degree at a polytechnic as well as at a university. In the other two countries this is not possible: a diploma that is awarded by a Dutch and German polytechnic cannot be awarded by a university, and vice versa. Another main difference with which we were confronted is that in the United Kingdom many more part-time students are participating in higher education than in the Netherlands. In other words it can be assumed that the work experience of the students in the United Kingdom is considerably larger than in the Netherlands. The question then becomes to what extent this will have consequences for the output in terms of the quality of graduates?

Differences between higher education systems lead to some methodological and practical problems. In the first place there is the language and transfer problem. A valid comparison requires definitions of terms to more or less guarantee that peers do not talk at cross-purposes. When, for example, they discuss a part of the study programme it is important to know whether they have in mind a 'course', a 'subject', or a 'unit'. All these can have different meanings. The general question therefore is whether all educational terms can be translated into a sort of universal language, so that there will be no misunderstanding.

Another problem is the availability and accessibility of data. This is especially the case with information about graduates in the labour market. At the higher education institutions in two of the three countries there is no tradition of monitoring the graduates when they leave the institution.

This problem also arises with respect to the tradition of quality assessment in the three countries. We knew beforehand that the Netherlands and the United Kingdom differ from Germany. Both the Netherlands and the United Kingdom have established procedures for quality assessment, eg the CNAA validation and the VSNU and HBO Council visiting committees. However, no formalised procedures of this kind exist in Germany. Although we do not want to suggest that because of the existence or non-existence of such procedures any conclusions can be formulated *a priori* regarding differences in quality between these countries, it became apparent that they have had marked effects on the availability of data. Both in the Netherlands and in the United Kingdom extensive data were available at the institutional level on both programmes (structure and contents) and student achievements. In Germany, this kind of information proved harder to come by. In particular, institutional level data turned out to be something of a problem. Or, phrased differently, there was less of a tradition of systematic data gathering at the institutional level in Germany. We therefore believe it fair to conclude, again without making any comments on the quality of institutional performance, that it appears that the existence of institutionalised quality assessment procedures results in the availability of process and output related data at the institutional level.

4.3 Preliminary results of the data

We argued before that the performance indicator kind of data we attempted to collect would primarily be used as an input for the peer review process, and not for making sec comparisons. We still hold this opinion, but it should be qualified somewhat. Certainly at the system level, data can be compared rather straightforwardly without the problem of 'contextual distortion'. Based on the results of the data collection (phase 1), the following comparative statements can be made for the dimensions previously discerned, highlighting the similarities and differences between the three countries.

4.3.1 Structure of the systems

With respect to primary and secondary education it can be noted that formally Dutch children spend 14 years in school before enrolling at a university, while in Germany and the United Kingdom this is 13 years. Also, British and Dutch students, because of the structure of the educational system, can enrol at the age of 18, while in Germany they are at least 19. German children start their formal education at the age of six, while in the United Kingdom and the Netherlands they do so at the age of, respectively, five and four.

In regard to pre-university secondary education, it can be noted that the British system leads to an earlier specialisation in terms of subject fields than is the case in Germany and the Netherlands. In general, British pupils take their GCSE examinations at the age of 16, after which they specialise in two or three fields for which they take the A-level examinations at the age of 18. In the Netherlands pupils take their final pre-university examinations (consisting of seven subjects) at the age of 18, while in Germany students take the final examination (either a general or a subject-specific one) at the age of 19. No two-stage process exists in these countries.

With respect to the higher education structure, it should be noted that the British structure differs markedly from the Dutch and German one. In the United Kingdom a distinction can be made between the Bachelor's and the Master's degree, whereby the Bachelor's degree can be obtained after on average three years of study and can be followed by a Master's degree after a further one or two years of study. The Bachelor's degree is a full degree, in the sense that it is considered to be a final qualification that is recognised by the labour market. In the Dutch and German systems a distinction can also be made in two phases, namely the *propaedeutic* and *doctoral* phases in the Netherlands and the *Grundstudium* and *Hauptstudium* in Germany, but these are not considered to be final qualifications and are not recognised by the labour market. In Germany, the initial phase takes two years to complete, in the Netherlands one year. The final phase takes three years to complete in the Netherlands and two to two and a half years in Germany. Formally therefore, not much difference can be observed in terms of length of study between these two countries. However, in practice these differences are substantial (see section 4.3.3).

4.3.2 Input features; admission, selection and age

The basic difference between, on the one hand, the British system and the Dutch and German one on the other, is the fact that British institutions can select their students, while in Germany and the Netherlands the pre-university qualification entitles a student to enrol at a university of his or her preference.

In the United Kingdom and the Netherlands, students generally enrol at a university usually straight from secondary education. Therefore, in general students are under 19 years of age when they enrol. In Germany, however, the 'alternative routes' to higher education are far more common. Approximately half the student population either accumulates working experience or combines work with education ('Berufsbildung') before enrolling at a university. This implies that the average age of first-year students is substantially higher (21.7 years); a situation quite similar to that of many students at the British polytechnics.

4.3.3 Process features; actual length of study, and completion

As indicated above, substantial differences can be observed regarding the actual time students take to complete their university education. In the United Kingdom, a student takes either three or four years to complete the Bachelor's degree, depending on the programme. Approximately 85% finish their degree within this three to four year period. In contrast, both Germany and the Netherlands show a marked difference between formal and actual length of study. In the Netherlands, the average student takes some 5.7 years to complete the degree, while in Germany the average length of study is between 7 and 7.5 years.

Data on completion rates are difficult to obtain, as output data have to be related to actual enrolment years. Most of the time this is not possible. Based on the limited data available for the three countries in this respect, it would seem that in the United Kingdom completion rates are somewhat higher than in the other two countries. However, such a conclusion has to be interpreted very carefully.

The above conclusions are, of course, not shocking. They are, or should be, known to those involved in comparative higher education research. Nevertheless, this kind of straightforward comparison has proved to be helpful as essential background information and as a starting point for formulating questions regarding the comparability issue in the peer review. As will be shown in the next chapter, these 'structural differences and similarities' featured prominently in the outcomes of the peer review process.

5 The international peer review

5.1 Identification of the peers

As indicated in Chapter 3, the envisaged peer group for the economics review consisted of two groups: an internal group with representation from the economics faculties selected as cases for this study, and an external group unrelated to the respective institutions. Identification of the members of the internal group was straightforward. After the consent from the selected faculties to participate in the project (in all cases readily given), they were asked to nominate a member for the review. In this way, identification of the internal peers has been based on 'self-selection' and resulted in the group consisting of both economists and educationalists with intimate knowledge of the programmes.

With respect to the external group, it was decided beforehand that this group should consist of both academics from the economics higher education community and representatives from the economics profession outside of higher education. In this way it was believed a diverse input in terms of expertise and experience with economics programmes and their graduates would be guaranteed. It was decided that because of both logistics and 'even representation' of the groups, the external group should consist of three members per country: two from within the academic community and one from the professional field. Identification of the peers proceeded from a peer process itself. Experts in the economics discipline were approached to identify peers based on the following (broad) criteria: a sound knowledge of the economics discipline, a good reputation within the discipline, preferably diverse professional experience and international experience with the higher education systems and study programmes in question. From the names provided by the experts, the peers were approached to obtain their co-operation for the review. The resulting peer groups are listed in Appendix I.

5.2 Preparation of the peer review

Before the actual peer review took place, the participants were given a structured set of information collected on the basis of the checklist (see Chapter 4). Volume I of this set contained the systems level information for the three countries together with an introduction on the aims and method of the project. Volume IIA contained the economics discipline level description for the three countries, and is included as Appendix II to this report. Next to these sets of - more or less background - information, the participants received detailed information on the economics programmes of the 10 faculties that were chosen as case studies. For each faculty, this included an overview of the economics programme under study, and detailed programme information on macro/micro-economics, quantitative methods and selected options in the final stage of the programme for specialisation in research/professional economics, financial services, quantitative economics and international economics. Apart from information on the content of the programmes (goals, objectives, reading lists, study-load, etc) examples of examination papers were included. Because of the sheer size of these volumes Appendix II contains only an overview of the contents. Further background information on the institutions, faculty, staff, student achievement (examples of final theses), etc was available for reference at the actual review.

5.3 The proceedings of the peer review

The peer review on economics took place on 15-17 July 1991 in Utrecht, the Netherlands. The first (half) day consisted of a preparatory briefing session with the designated chairs of the internal and external groups, an informal meeting session for the peers and a general briefing and introduction session. During the preparatory briefing session the project team discussed the detailed programme of the review with the chairs and further clarified the objectives of the review meeting. In the general briefing session the objectives of the review were again discussed based on the briefing note the members received with their documentation set. Amongst other things, it was emphasised that they were participating in a pilot project, and that the 10 study programmes involved were to be seen as typical for the higher education system in their respective countries. Furthermore, ample time was reserved for questions so as to overcome possible misunderstandings regarding the aims and objectives.

On the second day of the review, the two groups discussed the respective economics programmes according to the following format. In the first session, attention was focused on the structural features and the aims, contents, and teaching and assessment methods of the programmes involved. After this more or less general session, the second half of the morning was devoted to the core curriculum of the economics programmes (micro, macro and quantitative economics). In particular, the peers concentrated on:

- variations in the breadth, depth and focus of the curriculum;
- academic levels at the start and finish of the programmes;
- learning outcomes: eg oral or written competencies, computing (related to teaching and assessment methods and practical work);
- the balance and content of core subjects (where these exist) in relation to options.

In the afternoon, the third session was reserved for the options within the various economics programmes. By focusing on: (a) research/professional economics; (b) financial services; (c) quantitative economics; and (d) international economics, the peers discussed the extent of opportunities for specialist studies in the 10 programmes.

In the final session of the day, the peers were invited to formulate their overall conclusions with respect to the (academic) comparability of the programmes under review. From the four sessions, the secretariat produced short reports on the main conclusions of the two groups. These reports were distributed among the peers during the evening and formed the input for the final sessions on the third day.

The last day of the peer review consisted of two general sessions. First, the distinguishing features of the economics programmes in the three countries were discussed. The two summary reports on the findings of the internal and external group were commented on and compared.

Based on this, an attempt was made to formulate several general conclusions regarding the contents of the peer review. The second session was of an evaluative nature. The peers commented on the proceedings and viability of both the review and the overall method underlying the project.

It was agreed that the project team would draft the report on the peer review, which would then be distributed among the peers for comment and consent. In September 1991, the draft report was sent to the peers. On the basis of their comments and suggestions, the final report was completed in November 1991.

5.4 The outcomes of the peer review

The *output* of the peer review, ie the full peer report, is attached as Appendix I. We shall not go into the details of the conclusions regarding economics here, but instead concentrate on the *outcome* of the peer review. That is, we shall try to evaluate *how* the teams of peers operated and *what kind of conclusions* they reached.

Following the briefing session and the informal meeting on the first day, on the second day the groups quickly organised themselves and started discussions on the designated questions. The degree of concentration of the discussion was, accordingly, very satisfactory.

During the second day, a most striking feature was the extent to which the data set was used. Although probably due to accidental origins (late delivery), it was remarkable that the written data were used sparsely. Also, the extended data set present during the meetings was hardly consulted. Previous experience, especially the CNAA experience in the United Kingdom, had made us expect that peers use such data fairly extensively. Moreover, the design of the meeting had been thought to be conducive to extensive use of the data. In both sub-groups for each of the four subjects mentioned above, one person was designated (by the peer groups themselves) to draft and present a first comment, under explicit referral to the data set.

Relying, therefore, mostly on their own experience, it is not surprising that a certain case's (in the 'internal' group) or a certain country's (in the 'external' group) higher education structure to a large extent defined the peers' attitudes towards the subjects of discussion. Other cases or other countries were compared with what was - sometimes obviously - perceived to be the 'normal' way and level of teaching economics, where 'normal' is meant both in the positive sense (how it is *mostly* done) and in the normative sense (how it *ought* to be done). Nevertheless, this mostly resulted in a fairly balanced discussion, and fairly balanced conclusions. In other words: the peers tended to use their own situation (institution or country) as the frame of reference that provided them with the perspective to perceive and value other study programmes.

Regarding the conclusions, they are limited almost entirely to comparisons of the study programmes, not of their output (graduates). In some places, evaluative judgements are made beyond the comparisons. These statements too pertained mostly to the study programmes. Regarding the reasons for this focus, attention will be given to some extra-educational factors in Chapter 6. Here, we shall concentrate on the educational factors. Very important in this respect is the conclusion alluded to in sections 4.2, 4.3 and 11.1 of the peer report the data available are not sufficient to compare the levels of accomplishments of graduates from the different countries. This results both from the differences in structure and content of the study programmes under consideration and from personal characteristics of the students (eg the difference in age of German and UK graduates). Not only were such data not available in the present instance, they also do not exist. Hence the need mentioned in conclusion 12.2, *ii*, of the peer report to complement a project like this one with other types of research where output factors are more focused upon. The result of this was, however, that the peer groups did not make a connection between the characteristics of the educational process (content and structure of study programmes) and characteristics of graduates (level of knowledge, scientific or analytical attitude, or other academic skills and achievements), which had been a prime assumption of the design employed in this project.

As a result of the different backgrounds of the peers (regarding both countries and internal and external positions), we think a balanced view of the study programmes in the three countries has been obtained. The within-country differences have not been undervalued (witness the last conclusion in the peer report), yet several system-wide conclusions have also been drawn (section 12). Given the limitations mentioned before, the peer review has been a valuable exercise in the comparison of study programmes.

6 Evaluation of the international comparative method

6.1 Introduction

The central question to be addressed in this final chapter is, of course, what we have learned from the project about the applicability of the methodology used. To recapitulate, the project has been designed as a pilot study to assess the possibility of providing valid and reliable comparisons of the quality of higher education in several European countries. This goal has been specified in the central research question:

Which instruments, procedures, and additional means exist to make valid comparisons of the quality of higher education in different countries

The question stresses the fact that it is not the comparison of quality as such, but the methodological problems and pitfalls of international comparative assessments that are the key ingredients for the study. An attempt to overcome the known problems of comparisons across countries has been made by developing a two-stage procedure, combining elements of peer review and performance indicator approaches. A multiple procedure has been chosen because of the inherent weaknesses of the separate use of indicators or reviews. Stage one consisted of the development of a checklist identifying input, process, output and context features of the national system, the discipline and the study programme in question. Based on this checklist, data have been collected to be used as the input for stage two: the international peer review. The objective of the peer review has been the identification of commonalities and differences in the economics study programmes in the three countries. Therefore, the purpose has not been to see which study programmes are 'best'. Differences between the three higher education systems in terms of, eg length, structure and goals preclude such possibilities. However, it is entirely plausible to suggest that some programmes are better at some things than others and that some differences reflect system features as well as institutional ones.

The extent to which the methodology developed made it possible to reach these kind of conclusions will be discussed next. With respect to the two phases of the project, attention is first paid to the peer review, as its process and outcomes can be considered the final test for the viability of the method. In doing so, the peer review meeting will be addressed first, both from the participants' and from the research point of view. Later in this chapter, phase one will be analysed, especially in connection with the question of the extent it was instrumental for phase two.

6.2 Peers' experiences

The reactions of the experts involved in the peer review meeting were gathered in several ways. First, an evaluation form (see Appendix III) was handed out during the meeting, which was returned by 13 of the 17 participants (seven from the internal, six from the external group).[26] Also, reactions were invited to the draft version of the peer review report, mailed to the participants afterwards. Finally, there were informal reactions, both during the meeting and afterwards. On the basis of these sources the following can be said about the participants' assessment of the meeting.

6.2.1 Goals and the peer meeting

The fact that the peer review did have certain objectives does not imply by definition that these objectives are shared by the participants in the review. In order to obtain a broad picture of what motivated the peers in the review, they were asked in the questionnaire to list the aspects they considered important or unimportant. The aspects the participants viewed as most important about the meeting were: (a) gaining insight into the way economics is taught in other countries; and (b) meeting colleagues from those countries. Making statements about the quality of curricula and the quality of graduates in an international context was conceived as important by most, but not all participants. Other reasons (insight in to other curricula in one's country, meeting colleagues from one's own country) were important to not more than half the participants, or (visiting the venue) not important at all. The fact that getting to know curricula and economists from other countries was more often seen as important than the researchers' primary purpose with the meeting (reaching comparative quality judgements), may correlate with the kind of statements made by the peers. Those statements are more in the nature of comparisons about curricula, than in the nature of quality judgements. In this respect, the outcome of the pilot project has been altered to a certain extent because of the goals of the peers.

How can this be explained? In the first place, it is presumed, participants' initial interests were more in building or maintaining their international networks than in our research interest. This is a legitimate objective, of course, but one that may have been somewhat detrimental to the research project as far as it was aimed at leading to quality judgements about study programmes and, one step removed, graduates. A second factor was the absence of any clear outcome to the review. No decisions concerning any of the 10 programmes would be made on the basis of the results of the review. Therefore, nothing fundamental was at stake. The approach of the peers to the review reflected this fact.

For both explanations, however, it appears there is little one can do to overcome them. Personal agendas are a fact of life and certainly in a case where people invest a good deal of their limited time and energy on a very voluntary basis this can hardly be criticised. And pilot projects of this nature simply do have the, perhaps negative, element of no-strings-attached participation compared with actual review processes.

6.2.2 The data set

Another partial explanation for the peers not sharing the researchers' goals exactly may be found in the shortcomings in the preparation of the meeting. First, only half the participants thought the goal of the meeting had been clear to them before the meeting, though most felt they were better informed once they were assembled. In this respect, the general briefing session during the first day proved to be a valuable part of the review programme. Second, although all respondents had received Volume I of the documentation (system descriptions) before the meeting, about one quarter of them had not received the complete documentation set. The reason for this was, mostly, inaccuracy or slowness of delivery by the courier service employed. This was instrumental in not everyone reading all of the material beforehand. Other reasons for this may have been the intricate organisation of the documentation set and its sheer Volume. Nevertheless, participants as a rule indicated they had read the core information (Volume I) and, often, the descriptions of discipline-wide features (Volume IIA) thoroughly. However, the actual case descriptions (Volumes IIB-D) received less attention in the peers' preparation for the review.

The perceptions of the quality of the information contained in the data set varied. In a few cases it was thought that the descriptions pertaining to other countries were well enough, but those pertaining to the respondent's own country were 'improvable'. Possibly this means our descriptions are more condensed, not as detailed as a country's representative would have wished - which was precisely what we aimed at: a concise, but truthful description of general trends and principles, not an exhaustive picture of all particular facts. In some cases other countries' descriptions were not well thought of; however, a specific pattern could not be found in these responses. Almost half the respondents thought all descriptions were equally good, and almost everyone found the descriptions at least partly comparable (on all levels: from country-wide to case-specific).

Again, almost all respondents found the data set important in terms of forming opinions about the economics curricula. One respondent judged it to be possible to make the same kind of statements without the written material. Also, one respondent found Volume I and Volume IIA to be of low importance. In the case-specific descriptions (Volumes IIB-D), everyone rated the course structure data of at least medium importance, and only a small minority valued the other information less than that (specific information on micro and macro-economics, on quantitative methods and on the specialist strands). With respect to the peers' assessment of Volumes IIB-D the attention they gave to these Volumes somewhat qualifies their judgement as expressed through the questionnaire.

In sum, more timely delivery of the data set, more immediately comprehensible organisation and a further reduction of the data might have been helpful in making the data gathered in phase one of the project more useful in phase two. Nevertheless, most peers had read an important part of the material and, in terms of the content, thought it useful, even important, for their forming an opinion.

6.2.3 Effectiveness of the peer review meeting

The peers' opinions on the effectiveness of the review were almost unanimous: the purpose of the meeting was partly fulfilled. (Very small minorities of the 'internal' group are either more positive or less positive.) Only one respondent judged it to be possible to make the same kind of statements based only on the written material.

When faced with several alternative methods of organising a peer review, however, none of the respondents opted for a single plenary meeting as had been the design for this particular review. Some respondents preferred a procedure including site visits, but the majority preferred a number of plenary meetings. From this we conclude that more time should be given for a detailed exchange of information between the peers than proved to be possible during the July meeting on economics.

Regarding the composition of the peer group that would be desirable according to the present peers, the respondents' opinions were split almost 50-50 on the inclusion of all alternatives mentioned (independent experts from higher education, professionals or university staff from participating institutions) save one: a clear majority did not think other types of individuals than those mentioned should be included. Among the other types of individuals suggested by the minority were students. In addition, the usefulness of other viewpoints, especially employer feedback, was emphasised in the peers' comments.

The peers' remarks about the project as such contained, among others, appeals to extend this to a 'real' research project, leading to evaluations of the material based on hypotheses by researchers before putting it to the scrutiny of peers. Other suggestions included bringing more (EC) countries into the project, and to have some (unspecified) form of follow-up.

Among the more critical remarks stood out those that emphasised that the discussion had been much more about the educational process than about its effects on students, and that the discussion had been a mixture of 'is' and 'ought' statements. In other words, the critique was directed at the way the discussions had proceeded, not on the usefulness of the meeting itself.

To summarise, the meeting has in the eyes of the participants, only partly reached its objectives. The majority think a group of about the same composition as theirs, in a series of meetings, could reach more satisfactory comparative quality judgements. The basis of the written material should be more prestructured than it was now, eg by the researchers adding evaluation statements *before* sending the material to the peers. In that case, a more focused discussion on the evaluative statements made by the researchers would be possible.

6.3 A critique of the peer review

Apart from the peers' views of the peer review meeting, our conclusions are that the strengths and weaknesses of the peer review as implemented in this project are the same for international purposes as its strengths and weaknesses generally.[27]

Its major strengths derive from the knowledge and experience that are brought to bear on the process and hence the authority that derives from the resultant judgements. The latter, we believe, have a robustness, credibility and legitimacy that bureaucratic or performance indicator approaches, for example, are unlikely to attain. Equally though, there is always a danger that the judgements do not provide the kind of clear-cut picture of reality decision-makers require. The peer review meeting also revealed another of the strengths of the method - its potential contribution to quality enhancement through the exchange of ideas and information.

It should not be forgotten, however, that peer review is a social process. The inherent subjectivity of the method necessarily means that the outcome of any particular peer review is influenced by the specific individuals involved and by the interactions among them. Although the use of a group of individuals and the expectation of rational argumentation as a rule ensure that broadly the same statements follow from different peer reviews of the same object, the subjective aspects mean that exact replication cannot be expected. From this follow the weaknesses that became evident in this meeting, and which are also the weaknesses of peer review more generally: the tendency for self-interests to intrude (whether personal, institutional or, as in this case, national) and the difficulty of assessing learning outcomes and hence academic levels. It was the latter that we felt was the major failure of this peer review: the inability to reach the same firmness of conclusion about quality and academic level as was achieved with respect to curriculum comparisons. The need to augment peer review of this sort by methods that provide a more direct indication of outcomes and levels was a major conclusion of the review. Possible methods might include, on the output side, employer inputs and graduate feedback, or on the process aspect, external examiners or 'blind' marking of sample assessments from the three countries by another international panel.

In comparing quality in higher education, there is often ambiguity about whether one is comparing programmes of study or the outcomes of these programmes, ie what graduates have learned. As argued before, in this project the emphasis has been on the programmes, as the single most important factor also and the one that can be manipulated by university staff. Clearly, however, the programme of study is not the factor that explains most of the outcome. Many other factors also influence the characteristics, skills and abilities of a graduate: previous educational experience (length, structure and level of primary and secondary education); experience before and during the study in other societal aspects; upbringing by the student's parents; genetic characteristics, etc. Yet in relation to the study programme, the international panel did reach a broad consensus about what a degree-level programme in economics should contain in general terms - at least in the three countries involved - and thereby provided a comparator against which other economics study programmes might be judged.

The previous sentence was deliberately put in terms of study programmes, for if one thing transpired in this peer review, it was that the within-country differences were so large as to make it difficult to assume the national level to be homogeneous enough to use it as the level of comparison. On the contrary, the operative aims of study programmes and the kinds and levels of accomplishments expected from graduates varied significantly within each country. Therefore, the appropriate level of comparison appears to be the study programme level rather than the national level. The emphasis put on the programme level data in Figure 1 is confirmed by this experience, and the national and discipline levels should, even more than now, be conceived of as boundary conditions. They influence, but do not determine, the study programmes and the outcomes.

6.4 Evaluation of the data collection phase

In the light of the peer review and its results some comments can be made about phase one of the project. For the information collected was, in the first instance, intended to be instrumental for the second phase.

6.4.1 Conclusions from the peer review for an extended study

The relevant questions from this point of view are on redundant and missing data. Which available information was not used and which information was desired by the peers but was not available?

The first remark we can make here is that the quantity of information available was more than sufficient. Not all of the information gathered was used. Therefore, in an eventual sequel, phase one could be shorter and more efficient. This implies that less information should be gathered, leaving out those sections that were not important to the process. Also, it could mean a restructuring of the checklist so as to make it more easily comprehensible to the peers. Which dimensions of the checklist could be deleted or 'streamlined' depends on whether this sequel would be a repetition, ie in fact geared to programme comparison, or would have a different focus. To the latter possibility we shall return in the next sub-section, but for the moment we assume the goal to remain identical.

The parts of information that were read most by the peers and that were the most important to their minds, according to the evaluation forms, were the nation-wide descriptions of the higher education systems. This, in our view, attests to the importance of the national systems as boundary conditions, since the discussions were more about specific programmes (in both groups of peers) than about national higher education systems as such. Moreover, parts of these descriptions were not used at all in the discussions. Therefore, the information about forms of teaching and assessment, for example, can be omitted from the national level part of the checklist henceforth. The discipline level of information could, for the same reasons, be 'slimmed' in a similar way, though to a lesser extent. In this manner, both the quantity of information can be diminished and the extent to which it is focused on the target of it all, the programme level, can be improved. Especially, the information about programme structures was seen to be important at this level, more so than the even more detailed analysis on specific topics (entry and exit levels of core elements and skills, and special strands). Reduction of the latter type of information could, therefore, also be considered. An additional advantage of the latter, apart from a substantial reduction of the data set, would be a very large reduction of the time needed to collect and sort this kind of information, enhancing the efficiency of the method.

More information, on the contrary, would be needed about the actual levels of attainment[28] of students - not so much in specialist strands, but in the mainstream of the study programme under consideration. This would require, for instance, not just examination questions, as were collected this time, but also information on standards of judgement. The level of attainment is an essential factor in any (international) comparison leading to quality judgements. At the same time it is one of the most difficult ones from a research perspective. The method used in this project clearly indicated that extensive data collection at the programme level and judgement by peers does not solve the problem. Further research in this critical area is needed if quality comparisons are to extend beyond the comparison of curricula.

6.4.2 Other aims and other information

If a sequel to the project were to be geared toward other aims than programme comparison, other information would be needed. Specifically, so as to focus the peers more toward quality judgements than toward programme comparisons, less detailed programme information should be given beforehand. As the study programmes nevertheless remain the 'empirical basis' of at least part of graduates' qualities, the type of information gathered in Volumes IIB - D should be made available at the meeting (accompanied by, eg a research fellow who, when appropriate, could point out to the peers that certain information is available).

The suggestion made in the last paragraph of the previous section, that more information about actual levels of attainment should be gathered, can be repeated here. It would be even more important to this goal.

Another suggestion made before that we would like to repeat here concerns other types of information. Especially, more information about the 'outcome' of the educational process would be welcome, such as feedback from graduates (satisfaction from the point of view of their success on the labour market, or from the point of view of personal fulfilment), from professionals working in the non-higher education field, from employers, etc, would be needed. A modest attempt has already been made in this project to present job market information and to represent the professional field in the peer group, but much more emphasis on these aspects would be needed in a sequel. This might mean substantial investments would have to be made in this kind of research, eg in graduate surveys or employer interviews.[29]

In connection to the above, several suggestions were made to use 'case law' resulting out of the existence and growth of the Erasmus networks. In these networks, actual comparisons of quality are made to some extent, as decisions are made in which part of the programme offered by the host institution or faculty foreign students can enrol. This indeed appears to be a valid suggestion, as data of this kind could quite easily be obtained through the network documentation. Also, student perceptions on the quality of the programmes and the administration of exams could be obtained through questionnaires. The results of such an exercise should, however, be interpreted with some care, as an element of self-selection exists. It would appear likely that especially the best students would opt for a period of study in another country. Their responses could therefore be somewhat different from those of the 'average student'.

Finally, the point bears repetition that, whatever the exact aims of a sequel project, it should be geared exclusively to the study programme level as far as its conclusions and judgements are concerned. Since the within-country differences proved to be anything but negligible, a higher level of abstraction is not justified. European higher education quality is produced in individual graduates with the aid of individual study programmes, therefore it is either the individuals or the programmes that should be assessed regarding their quality. The highest possible level, and the most efficient, is, then, to assess study programmes.

Notes

1 ARHO, 1989.
2 ARHO, 1989: p24.
3 NUFFIC, 1990.
4 From: OECD, 1990: p6.
5 See also: Westerheijden, D F & P A M Maassen, 1991.
6 See *Der Spiegel*, December 1990.
7 See also: Frackmann, E, 1991.
8 Pirsig, 1974: 163.
9 Popper, K R, 1965 (1963), p20.
10 Ball 1985.
11 Cave *et al*, 1988: 17 *ff*.
12 Segers, Dochy & Wijnen, 1989: 2–3.
13 For the different criteria in different disciplines, see also: Becher, 1989.
14 Rigter, 1983.
15 See also: De Weert 1990: p65.
16 Cave *et al.*, 1988: esp. pp63–72; Sizer, 1989: pp17–20.
17 Sizer, 1989: 20; Cave *et al*, 1988: 57, 78.
18 De Weert, 1990: pp64–66.
19 Boyer, cited in: De Weert, 1990: p64.
20 See also: De Weert, 1990: pp65–66.
21 Blume & Sinclair, 1973; see also: Brennan, 1990.
22 Eg: Cole, Cole & Simon, 1981.
23 NUFFIC, 1990.
24 See also: De Vree, 1982.
25 A recent effort at ranking higher education institutions (*per discipline!*) has been made by *Libération*, December 1989.
26 Because of the small numbers, quantitative analysis of the evaluation forms is hardly appropriate.
27 See also, eg: Westerheijden, D F, 1991.
28 On problems of defining 'levels' in study programmes, see, eg, Gottschal 1991. Note, however, that Gottschal tries to define such levels, while in peer review it is assumed that the peers, albeit perhaps implicitly, know how to do so.
29 See also several modules in the CHEPS Quality Assessment Data Package.

References

General References

ARHO, 1989: *Europa 1992 en het Nederlandse hoger onderwijs [Europe 1992 and Dutch higher education]*. Den Haag: ARHO.

Ball, C, 1985: *Fitness for Purpose*. Guildford: SRHE & NFER-Nelson.

Blume, S S & Sinclair, R, 1973: 'Chemists in British universities: A study in the reward system of science', *American Sociological Review*, 38: 126.

Brennan, J, 1990: 'A non-university perspective of quality assessment in the United Kingdom', in Goedegebuure, L C J, Maassen, P A M & Westerheijden, D F (eds), 1990: *Peer review and performance indicators: quality assessment in higher education in Great Britain and the Netherlands*. Culemborg: Lemma.

Cave, M, Hanney, S, Kogan, M & Trevett, G, 1988: *The use of performance indicators in higher education*. London: Jessica Kingsley.

Cole, S, Cole, J R & Simon, G A, 1981: 'Chance and consensus in peer review', *Science*

De Vree, J K, 1982: *Foundations of social and political processes*. Bilthoven: Prime Press.

Goedegebuure, L C J, Maassen, P A M & Westerheijden, D F (eds), 1990 *Peer review and performance indicators: quality assessment in higher education in Great Britain and the Netherlands*. Culemborg: Lemma.

Gottschal, P, 1992: *Niveaus en de pluriformiteit van het hoger onderwijs. Over het vergelijken van curricula. [Levels and the pluriformity of higher education. On comparison of curricula.]* Den Haag: NUFFIC.

NUFFIC, 1990: *Waardering van kwaliteit: internationale erkenning en waardering van het Nederlandse Hoger Onderwijs [Valuation of quality: international recognition and valuation of Dutch higher education]*. Den Haag: NUFFIC.

OECD, 1990: *Review of educational policy in the Netherlands*. Paris: OECD.

Pirsig, R M, 1974: *Zen and the art of motorcycle maintenance*. New York: Morrow.

Popper, K R, 1965 (1963): *Conjectures and refutations*. New York: Harper & Row.

Rigter, H, 1983: *De prestaties van het Nederlandse gezondheidsonderzoek [The performance of Dutch health research]*. Den Haag: RAWB.

Segers, M S R, Dochy, F J R C & Wijnen, W H F W, 1989: *Een set van prestatie-indicatoren voor de bestuurlijke omgang tussen overheid en instellingen voor hoger onderwijs [A set of performance indicators for the administrative relationships between the government and the higher education institutions]* Zoetermeer: Ministerie van Onderwijs & Wetenschappen.

Sizer, J, 1989: 'Performance indicators and quality control in higher education' in: McVicar, M (ed): *Performance indicators and quality control in higher education*. Portsmouth Polytechnic.

Weert, E de, 1990: 'A macro-analysis of quality assessment in higher education', *Higher Education*, 19: 57–72.

Westerheijden, D F, 1991: 'Promises, problems and pitfalls of peer review: the use of peer review in external quality assessment in higher education', Paper for the International Seminar on Assessing Quality in Higher Education, Bath, 16-19 July.

Westerheijden, D F & Maassen, P A M, 1991: 'Oriëntatie en selectie van studenten in Duitsland en Frankrijk' ['Orientation and selection of students in Germany and France'], in: *De rol van de propedeuse* [*The role of the first year of higher education*] Utrecht: VSNU.

References per country

Germany

Bock, K H, 1990: *Studien und berufswahl [Study and choice profession].* Bad Hannef.

Bundesministerium für Bildung und Wissenschaft (BMWB), 1989: *Das sociale Bild der Studentenschaft in den Bundes Republik Deutschland [The social image of the student community in Germany]* (84), Bonn: BMWB.

Bundesministerium für Bildung und Wissenschaft (BMWB), 1989: *Grund- und Strukturdaten [Basic data and structure data].* Bonn: BMWB.

Foreign Office of the Federal Republic Germany, 1982: *The educational system*, Köln: DAAD.

Frackman, E, 1990: 'Resistance to change or no need for change? The survival of German higher education in the 1990s', *European Journal of Education*, 25: 2.

Frackmann, E, 1991: 'Quality assurance in German Higher Education', paper for HIS.

The Netherlands

Bijleveld, R, 1990: 'Numeriek rendement en studieduur voor en na invoering van de wet twee-fasenstructuur', ['Completion rates and time to degree before and after implementation of the two tier structure'] *Tijdschrift voor hoger onderwijs* 8: 2.

Erasmus Universiteit Rotterdam, Faculteit der Economische Wetenschappen (FEW), *Zelfstudie economie en econometrie [Self-study economics and econometrics]* Rotterdam: FEW.

Goedegebuure, L C J, Maassen, P A M & Westerheijden, D F (eds), 1990: *Peer review and performance indicators: quality assessment in higher education in Great Britain and the Netherlands.* Culemborg: Lemma.

Kaiser, F, Koelman, J B J, Florax, R J G & Van Vught, F A, 1991: *Public expenditure on higher education; A comparative study in the EC-member states, 1975-1988.* Enschede: CHEPS.

Katholieke Universiteit Brabant, Faculteit der Economische Wetenschappen (FEW), 1990: *Zelfstudie ten behoeve van de externe visitatie [Self-study on behalf of the external visitation]* Tilburg: FEW.

Louw, R G (ed), 1989: *Wetgeving wetenschappelijk onderwijs [Legislation university education].* Den Haag.

Ministerie van Onderwijs & Wetenschappen, 1989: *Ontwerp hoger onderwijs- en onderzoeksplan (HOOP) [Draft higher education and research plan].* Den Haag: Staatsuitgeverij.

Ministerie van Onderwijs & Wetenschappen, 1989: *Ontwerp hoger onderwijs- en onderzoeksplan. HOOP) Feiten en cijfers [Draft higher education and research plan. Facts and figures].* Den Haag: Staatsuitgeverij.

Nijeboer, J J B, 1989: 'Verschillen academici en HBO-ers in beloning en arbeidsmarktposities', [Differences between HBO-ers and university graduates in recompense and position at the labour market] *Tijdschrift voor hoger onderwijs* 9: 4.

Rijksuniversiteit Groningen, Faculteit der Economische Wetenschappen (FEW),1990: *Zelfstudie economie en fiscale economie [Self-study economics and fiscal economics].* Groningen: FEW.

Vereniging van Samenwerkende Nederlandse Universiteiten (VSNU), 1987: *De kwaliteit van het universitair onderwijs [The quality of university education].* Utrecht: VSNU.

United Kingdom

Department of Education and Science, Welsh Office, 1985: *The Educational system of England and Wales.* London: DES, WO.

Department of Education and Science, 1989: *The English polytechnics - An HMI commentary.* London: DES.

Department of Education and Science, 1990: *Report of the review of the CNAA.* London: DES.

Government Statistical Service, 1989: *Education Statistics for the United Kingdom.* London: GSS.

HMSO, 1987, *Higher education - meeting the challenge* CM114, HMSO: London.

Central Services Unit/Association of Graduate Careers Advisory Services, 1989: *Summary of first destinations and employment of students.* London: CSU.

Turner, D & Pratt, J, 1990: Bidding for funds in higher education, *Higher Education Review* 22: 3.

Appendix I

Peer review report

Report of the peer review of economics programmes in Germany, the Netherlands and the United Kingdom
Held in Utrecht, the Netherlands, 15-17 July 1991

1 Introduction

1.1 — The panels for the peer review comprised economics specialists from the three participating countries with one group (the internal group) made up of economists and education staff members from the 10 study programmes under review and the other (the external group) consisting of independent economists drawn from the profession.

1.2 — Members of the internal panel were as follows:

Germany
Dr E Lachmann — Universität Köln, Wirtschafts- und Sozialwissenschaftliche Fakultät

The Netherlands
Drs H G van Liempd — Faculty of Economic Sciences, Catholic University, Brabant
Dr J A Ribbers — Faculty of Economics, Erasmus University, Rotterdam
Mrs drs M T Vugteveen — Faculty of Economics, University of Groningen

United Kingdom

Mr P Cooper — Department of Economics, Portsmouth Polytechnic
Prof B A Corry — Department of Economics, Queen Mary and Westfield College, London University
Dr F Green — Department of Economics, University of Leicester
Prof G Hadjimatheou — Head of Department of Economics, City of London Polytechnic

1.3 — Members of the external panel were as follows:

Germany
Prof Dr G Brinkman — Universität Siegen
Dr T Jendges — Technische Universität Berlin, Wirtschaftwissenschaftliche Fakultät
Dr K I Voigt — Universität Hamburg, Seminar fur Industriebetriebslehre

The Netherlands
Prof Dr W Albeda — Faculty of Economic Sciences, University Limburg
Prof Dr J G Backhaus — Faculty of Economic Sciences, University Limburg

| Mr I Verdouw | Director, Amsterdam Academy for Banking and Finance |

United Kingdom
The Lord Desai	Professor of Economics, London School of Economics and Political Science
Mr A Dilnot	Director, Institute of Fiscal Studies, London
Prof G Zis	Head of Department of Economics and Economic History, Manchester Polytechnic

1.4 — The internal panel was chaired by Professor B A Corry; the external panel was chaired by Professor Dr W Albeda.

1.5 — Economics programmes at the nine institutions listed above, together with the Universität Münster and the Universität Osnabruck, which were not represented at the meeting, were used as case studies. All of the programmes were from universities or university-equivalent institutions (ie the English polytechnics). The following documentation had been circulated to members in advance of the peer review meeting:

i An outline of the aims and methods of the project together with system descriptions for each of the three countries providing information on input, process, environmental and output features (*Volume I*).

ii An analysis of discipline-wide features and features of the individual study programmes in the three countries (*Volume II, A, B, C, and D*).

In addition, further information on each of the case study programmes, including staff and student details, was available to members at the meeting.

2 Organisation of the peer review

2.1 — On day one of the meeting, the participants were briefed about the purposes, aims and procedures of the peer review.

2.2 — The second day was organised in two parallel sessions, one consisting of the economics programme representatives (the internal group) and the other comprising the independent economists (the external group). At the end of the day a brief report summarising the deliberations of each group was prepared and circulated to all participants. On day three the groups met together to discuss the distinguishing features of economics programmes in each of the countries and other matters raised in each group's report. Finally, there was an evaluative session on the methodologies used with particular reference to the provision of documentation and the peer review process.

3 Focus for the peer review

3.1 — Three topics were discussed by each group on day two as follows: structural features of the programmes, the core curriculum and options, with each national group making a brief presentation under each of these headings. In the session devoted to structural features the emphasis was on the aims, contents, teaching approaches and assessment methods typified by the case studies selected for each country. Consideration of the core curriculum focused upon issues relating to level and content and to the balance between the core and the rest of the curriculum. Under options the extent of opportunities for specialist studies and more diversified pathways was explored.

4 General structural features

4.1 — The nominal length of study required to obtain a graduate qualification in economics in each of the three countries varies. In Germany the initial and second phases combined requires nine semesters (4.5 years), whereas in the Netherlands the requirement is four years (initial phase one year plus secondary phase three years). The United Kingdom requirement is three years.

4.2 — The UK first degree course is normally also completed in three years. Both Germany and the Netherlands differ from the UK in that the majority of students exceeded these nominal lengths of study, substantially so in the case of Germany. UK students were generally younger at entry and on graduation than their counterparts in the Netherlands and particularly in Germany. The view was expressed that German students were possibly disadvantaged in their future careers by the length of programmes and by their age on qualifying. On the other hand, their greater maturity could enable them to obtain greater intellectual benefits from their studies.

4.3 — An awareness of these differences led to much discussion about the levels attained by economics graduates in the three case study countries and this was a recurring theme throughout the second day. Some members considered that it would be more appropriate to compare Dutch and German graduate levels with those reached by UK students on completion of a Master's degree in economics which normally required one year's further full-time study after graduation. Others, however, felt that no such inference could be made on the basis of the evidence they had been asked to consider and that, without undertaking carefully designed and controlled experiments, any judgements made would necessarily be impressionistic.

4.4 — One general trend was, however, noted, namely the more students moved beyond the initial phase (year 1 in the UK and the Netherlands, year 2 in Germany) the more freedom they had to choose between options and specialisations.

4.5 — It was recognised that differences between the schooling systems impacted upon the content and level of the university programmes. Students entered programmes from a different base. Thus, UK programmes had to provide a general social science background in the first year of study which had already been obtained at secondary school in the other countries.

5 Course aims

5.1 — There was a consensus that the economics courses in the three countries focused (though with varying degrees of emphasis) on producing graduates who were adept at problem-solving using analytical techniques and intellectual skills derived from a study of the discipline, and who also had a broad and, in many cases, an international perspective on the subject.

5.2 — However, despite this broad comparability of aims, it was felt that programmes in Germany and the Netherlands appeared to be more oriented towards producing graduates who would become professional economists, whereas in the UK, at the undergraduate level, the emphasis was on general intellectual development through a study of economics. Members remained divided as to whether this difference of emphasis arose from within the programmes themselves or was due to exogenous factors, particularly those relating to differently structured labour markets for economists in Germany and the Netherlands compared with the UK.

6 Course Content

6.1 — Two important distinguishing features between the Netherlands and Germany on the one hand and the UK on the other were noted:

i The greater emphasis accorded to mathematics and quantitative methods on courses in Germany and the Netherlands, compared with the UK. This was felt to be due, in part at least, to the fact that many UK students have not studied mathematics beyond the age of 16 and that GCE 'A'-level mathematics is not generally a prerequisite for admission to UK economics degree courses.

ii Relations with neighbouring specialisms/disciplines of business economics and business studies/administration differed. Business *economics* programmes in the Netherlands and Germany, though clearly separate from general economics, were part of the discipline in terms of orientation and culture. In the UK *business studies* or *administration* programmes, economics was only one, and often a minor one, of several disciplinary inputs. Economics thus appeared to control different areas of curriculum territory in the three countries with implications for the focus and emphasis of the discipline.

6.2 — In addition, the following features were highlighted:

i The importance of law and, to a somewhat lesser degree, of political theory on economics courses in Germany and the general absence of these subjects from UK degree courses.

ii Law was a popular choice in the options part of economics programmes in the Netherlands.

iii The fact that year 1 economics courses in the UK frequently contained a broad ranging social sciences element which students in the Netherlands and Germany acquired at secondary school level.

iv Course components in the Netherlands and Germany were able to capitalise upon the foreign language competence of students at entry (particularly English-language proficiency) and this assisted the incorporation of an international and comparative dimension to all aspects of the curriculum. By contrast, it was rare for UK students of economics to be proficient in a foreign language at entry or to study a foreign language as part of the course.

6.3 — There was also an interesting discussion on the extent to which prospective students in the respective countries were: (a) well informed about the content of individual programmes; and (b) decided about career orientation prior to entry. It was suggested that Dutch students might be the best informed and most career decided, with UK students being the least informed and decided (due, most probably, to their younger age at entry and the more general aims of UK degree programmes in economics).

7 Teaching approaches

7.1 — It was agreed that teaching approaches were largely determined in each of the countries by practical matters such as student numbers, student-staff ratios, the availability of appropriate accommodation, etc. UK programmes of study typically involved much smaller and pre-selected cohorts of students than was the case in the Netherlands and Germany where access is much less controlled. This resulted in less reliance on 'magisterial' lectures in the UK, with more emphasis being given throughout the course to student-led seminars, workshop activities (particularly for information technology and quantitative methods) and self-directed study through project-based work. In the Netherlands and Germany very large lecture groups were common, particularly in the initial phase, with few formal opportunities for feedback from students. Seminar and group work did, however, become more widespread in the secondary phase and all three countries used postgraduate students as teaching assistants for these purposes. Individual tutorials and personal guidance and counselling tended to be restricted to the more elite system of the UK but, it was noted, these were coming under increasing pressure as student-staff ratios rose.

In Germany and the Netherlands approaches to teaching and assessment emphasised students' mastery of standard textbooks. This reliance on textbooks was not found in the UK, where even in the first year students rapidly developed the ability to use journals and articles, and conduct literature searches.

7.2 — In Germany and the Netherlands formal teaching contact hours appeared to be considerably higher than the 13 to 16 hours per week which seemed to be the norm in the UK. Thus, not only were they longer than the UK programmes, they were also more intensive. Possibly as a result, they appeared to be far more dependent on the use of set textbooks.

8 Assessment methods

8.1 — It was considered that UK programmes were characterised by a broader and more balanced range of forms of assessment, from course work assignments, projects and group work to more conventional unseen written examinations. In the Netherlands and Germany the right of students to progress beyond the initial phase was determined by performance in end-stage written examinations. In the Netherlands these sometimes took the form of multiple-choice questions. In the second phase, the Netherlands was the only country to make extensive use of *viva voce* examinations. While all three countries included project-based dissertations at the final stage, the practice tended to be less widespread in the UK and, where it occurred, also less ambitious in scope. In the Netherlands it was not unusual for project dissertations to be written in English.

8.2 — Two interesting observations, reflecting the influence assessment methods may have on approaches to learning, were made as follows:

i Because of the emphasis placed in Germany on *written* forms of assessment, it was felt that the oral competences of German students at the end of their course were inferior to the levels reached by their British and Dutch counterparts.

ii The competence of UK students in written assignments was considered to be higher in the initial phase of programmes; this was ascribed to traditions of assessed essays and projects in the sixth form of their secondary education.

9 Core curriculum

9.1 — There was agreement among members that a broadly similar core curriculum existed across the programmes under consideration and that this reflected current assumptions among most economists concerning what was key to the discipline. This core consisted of three major components: micro-economics, macro-economics and quantitative methods. The scope, depth of treatment and approach to each of these components were subject to variation not only from one national system to another but also from one institution to another, reflecting different programme aims and orientations and varied student backgrounds. This lack of homogeneity was considered to be an indicator of the continuing vitality of the discipline.

Nonetheless, the view was expressed that the proportion of the course overall taken up by core components seemed to be increasing.

9.2 — In all three countries core components must be passed as a necessary condition for progress to the next stage of the course.

9.3 — In addition, the following observations were made:

i It was generally the case that the proportion of the course overall represented by core components diminished as the course progressed.

ii What constituent elements made up each of the three core components, varies according to the particular pathway chosen by a student, eg general economics or business economics (in the Netherlands and Germany).

iii While, in all three countries, micro and macro-economics provide a solid theme for each course, the view was expressed that such a rigid division between the two may be questionable from both the conceptual and pedagogical standpoints.

iv The extent to which alternative paradigms are taught *through* the core components varied from course to course, though all programmes included some treatment of alternative paradigms in addition to neo-classical and Keynesian economics.

v Aspects of micro and macro-economics tended to be taught in relation to the national context in question, and this was generally felt to be important since students find it easier to apply principles to situations and systems with which they are relatively familiar.

vi Because of the tendency for broad-based first year courses in the UK, it was only in year 2 that core components began to figure prominently in courses and were treated in depth. This explains, in part at least, why some of the core textbooks - which tended to vary little from country to country - were recommended at earlier stages in the course in the Netherlands and Germany compared with the UK.

10 Options

10.1 — In all three countries there appeared to be an evolving menu of options on offer to students in the later stages of their courses. Choice of options available at any one time seemed to be determined by a combination of the following factors:

- market forces articulated in terms of student demand;
- professional views of what should be offered in economics degree programmes;
- the availability of local expertise and staff interests.

There was more opportunity for Dutch and German students to study options in subjects other than economics. After the foundation year, British students were generally limited to studies within the discipline of economics.

10.2 — Responsiveness to student demand tended to be the prime consideration at the present time, with the current trend being options relevant to finance, business and the service sectors. Institutions in all three countries were increasingly attempting to compile marketable packages which might prove attractive to students. However experience in the UK suggested that student choice was often influenced by teachers' abilities as much as by the content of options, about which students had little prior knowledge.

10.3 — Members stressed the importance of looking in detail at the content of options available to students through individual programmes. Option titles could be deceptive since a change of name was sometimes simply a cosmetic device to attract more students without a substantive change of course content.

10.4 — With regard to the range of options available in any one course, the need to distinguish between options which were freely available and those having prerequisites (particularly mathematics) was emphasised, as was the need to specify minimum student numbers for an option to run, and to monitor trends in this respect. The comparability of options within a programme also needed to be monitored carefully to preserve equity and maintain the quality and level of output.

10.5 — On the basis of the information and data received, it was not considered possible to make comparisons of the standards reached in options in the three countries under study. The shorter length of UK first degree courses might simply mean that *fewer* options were studied by

British students compared with their Dutch and German counterparts resulting in less breadth overall, but not necessarily less depth in individual components.

10.6 — It was noted that students in the Netherlands and the UK generally achieve better examination results in options compared with core components. Better results also tend to be achieved where the assessment is based significantly on course work rather than end of course examinations.

11 Other comments

11.1 — It was difficult to form a view about academic levels of attainment on the basis of written information in the form of course syllabuses, reading lists and sample examination papers. An approach based largely on input factors needs to be complemented by discussions with an appropriate range of employers of graduate economists in the three countries and graduates' retrospective views of their courses. It was recognised, however, that there might be a legitimate tension between the aims of higher education programmes and the specific vocational requirements of employers.

11.2 — The importance of the project/dissertation was emphasised by participants, particularly its potential in enabling students to appreciate the fundamental interconnectedness of the various strands of the economics curriculum. It also provided students with the opportunity to apply economics principles to 'real life' problems and situations.

11.3 — It was noted that the tendency had been for programmes of study in the Netherlands and Germany to be more loosely coupled than in the UK where the tendency had been towards highly structured and pre-specified programmes.

11.4 — Within each country, there is an assumption that universal standards are known and applied to programmes through mechanisms involving secondary marking and the external examiner system (which, for undergraduate courses, is unique to the UK). A suggestion was made that an experiment might be conducted to establish comparability of standards through inter-country external examiners.

11.5 — It was pointed out that 'case law' in respect of the comparability of standards between institutions in different countries is being built up through joint academic programmes and through institutional networks for mutual recognition. It was suggested that an inventory of such mechanisms might be established.

11.6 — Initiatives proposed in 11.4 and 11.5 might *inter alia* give some guidance to employers about the currency for the labour market of different academic qualifications.

11.7 — Some interesting variations were noted in the extent of movement between academic economists and industry, commerce and public life, and it was suggested that such movement might affect some areas of the delivery of economics programmes:

• There was little interchange in Germany, where teachers were career academics;

- There was considerable movement of staff in the UK from academic institutions outwards, but not in the reverse direction because of differentials in levels of remuneration;
- In the Netherlands, the level of interchange depended on the specialist areas of academic staff. There was movement between academic economists and trades unions, for example, and professorial staff could hold concurrent part-time appointments as members of company boards. In the area of finance, academics in the Netherlands did not have extensive contacts with the business world, and it was suggested that 'university banks' were needed on the analogy of university hospitals, to equip students to deal with the complex financial situations they might meet in employment.

12 Conclusions

12.1 — Much of the above report is by way of generalisation. Many of these generalisations permit exceptions even in the study programmes examined and certainly elsewhere in the three systems of higher education which we were looking at. This is even more true of the concluding points which follow. However, the peer review panel believes that they have a broad validity in terms of indicating differences in emphasis between the economics study programmes in the three countries.

12.2 — The following points are offered as general conclusions:

i   There is broad comparability between the content of economics study programmes to graduate level in the Netherlands, Germany and the United Kingdom; this is particularly true of the core curriculum components of micro and macro-economics and quantitative methods.

ii   Despite these similarities in content, differences in the length of programmes and in teaching and assessment methods are such as to suggest differences in learning outcomes. These could not be explored within the context of the peer review but the panel would recommend that this important issue is explored further using other methods.

iii   It did appear clear, however, that more attention to statistical and quantitative methods was generally given in the Dutch and German programmes and levels of student achievement in these areas were felt to be higher than in the United Kingdom.

iv   There are differences of emphasis in the objectives of economics programmes between the Netherlands and Germany on the one hand and the United Kingdom on the other. In the latter more importance was attached to economics as a vehicle for the general intellectual development of the student. Preparation of professional economists was reserved for a minority on masters programmes, ie a further year of study. This appears not be the case in Germany and the Netherlands. Graduates of the six Dutch and German study programmes would be regarded as professional economists and could expect to gain employment as such. UK graduates would not be in this position.

v   The above suggested to some members of the panel that a UK Master's programme in economics would have been a more suitable comparator for the study.

vi   The different national contexts provide important 'boundary conditions' in which teachers of economics have to work. The nature and length of secondary education and the available routes into higher education represent one important boundary condition; the use made of different educational qualifications in the labour market and the expectations of employers represent another. These affect study programmes in higher education through course aims and objectives and through the aspirations and expectations of entering students. Differences in learning outcomes are likely to result.

vii The generally lower age of UK students is an important factor conditioning the design and delivery or programmes in that country. The greater structuring of programmes and support for students is probably necessary to achieve desired learning outcomes with low levels of drop-out over the short three-year period. The broader experience and greater maturity of Dutch and German students are likely to affect their capacity to learn and the benefits they obtain from their study programmes. Panel members with experience of teaching students from more than one of the three countries could vouch that there were real differences.

viii The opportunity for students in the UK to study non-economics subjects beyond the foundation year appears to be much more limited than in the other countries. In Germany and the Netherlands, subjects such as law and political science have a continuing importance throughout the programme of study.

ix   There are evidently important differences within countries in respect of the above factors. In particular, the extent to which there is comparability in the learning outcomes - both in terms of content and level - across individual higher education institutions must be open to question.

Appendix II

Contents of the documentation
prepared for the peer review

Contents of Volumes I, II and III

Volume IIA Discipline-wide features and introduction to the case studies

Economics programmes in Germany

Economics programmes in the Netherlands

Economics programmes in the United Kingdom

Volume IIB Case studies Germany

Volume IIC Case studies The Netherlands

Volume IID Case studies United Kingdom

Volume III Additional information on study programmes

University of Leicester

Additional course information
Economics III core courses 1991-92
-   Economics of private and public choice
-   Growth, instability and uncertainty
-   Statistics III
-   Theory and applications of economic modelling
-   Examination papers
Labour economics
Business planning and decision making
Development of economic ideas

Exercises and practicals
Statistics I
Statistics II
Theory and practice of economic modelling

Background information
Degree courses in economics and business economics

Portsmouth Polytechnic

Additional course information
Economics workshop II
Economics analysis and policy
The dissertation

Examination papers
Computing for economists
Politics
Accounting and finance I
Economics analysis and policy
Development of economic ideas
Applied econometric modelling
Econometric methods
Industrial economics

Background information
Examination regulations
School of economics document
(staffing, research and consultancy, resourses, etc)

Queen Mary and Westfield College

Additional course information
3rd year industrial economics

Examination papers
Applied econometrics II

Exercises
Micro-economics I
Micro-economics II

Background information
Research report department of economics
Guide to undergraduate course structure and admissions

City of London Polytechnic

Additional course information
International economic growth since 1870
Britain since World War I
Public sector economics
Labour economics

Examination papers
The development of economic theory
The formation of economic enquiry (3x)
Economic and political framework
Britain since World War I (2x)

Background information
Research and staff development
Staffing details
Graduates employment details

Erasmus University Rotterdam

Additional course information
Economics course
– content of course
– flexibility of the studyprogramme
– type of educational interaction
– forms of assessment

Exercises
Macro-economics
Micro-economics

Background information
Fiscal economics
Econometrics

Catholic University of Brabant

Additional course information
Economics course
– content of course
– flexibility of the study-programme
– type of educational interaction
– forms of assessment

Exercises
Macro-economics

Background information
Fiscal economics
Econometrics

University of Groningen

Additional course information
Economics course
– content of course
– flexibility of the study-programme
– type of educational interaction
– forms of assessment

Exercises
Macro-economics
International economics

Background information
Fiscal economics
Econometrics

Universität zu Köln

Grund- und Hauptstudium (incl special fields)
Amtliche Mitteilungen (Studienordnung)

Background information
Amtliche Mitteilungen (Diplomprüfungsordnungen)

Westfälische Wilhelms Universität Münster

Additional course information
Studienplan und Studienordnung für den Studiengang Volkswirtschaftlehre
Kommentar zu den Vorlesungen: Grundstudium und Wirtschaftsinformatik (Wintersemester)
Kommentar zu den Vorlesungen: Grundstudium und Wirtschaftsinformatik (Sommersemester)
Kommentar zu den Vorlesungen: Hauptstudium (Wintersemester)
Kommentar zu den Vorlesungen: Hauptstudium (Sommersemester)

Other economics courses
Studienplan und Studienordnung für den Studiengang Betriebswirtschaftslehre
Ordnung im Studiengang Wirtschaftsinformatik

Universität Osnabrück

Additional course information
Studienordnung für den Studiengang Volkswirtschaftslehre
Prüfungsordnung für Diplom-Vlokswirt (Studiengang Volkswirtschaftslehre)

Other economics courses
Studienordnung für den Studiengang Betriebswirtschaftslehre
Prüfungsordnung für Diplom-Kauflaute (Studiengang Betriebswirtschaft)

Appendix III

Evaluation form for peer review

European quality: economics
Evaluation of peer review meeting, Utrecht, 15-17 July 1991

Preamble

This anonymous questionnaire is intended to help us evaluate the meeting of international experts in Economics, in Utrecht, 15-17 July 1991, and the previous phase of the European quality project, ie the collection and organisation of qualitative and quantitative data on economics study programmes in the participating countries.

We would appreciate it very much if you fill in this questionnaire and return it to the organisers before leaving Utrecht, or send it to CHEPS, to the attention of D F Westerheijden, at the address mentioned on this page.

The Research Team

A General

1 Please rate the following aspects as to their importance to you personally

	import-ant	neutral	unim-portant
Meet with colleagues from other countries	O	O	O
Meet with colleagues from (other) higher education institutions in my own country	O	O	O
Obtain insight into economics curricula in other countries	O	O	O
Obtain insight into economics curricula in (other) higher education institutions in my own country	O	O	O
The statements made about the quality of economics curricula in the three countries	O	O	O
The statements made about the quality of economics graduates in the three countries	O	O	O
To be in the Netherlands/Utrecht	O	O	O
Other:	O	O	O

2 Was the purpose of this meeting clear to you before you came to Utrecht?

yes	no
O	O

3 Was the purpose of the meeting clear to you during the meeting in Utrecht?

yes	no
O	O

B Preparation

1 Which parts of the material did you receive before the meeting?

	yes	no
Vol. I Countries	O	O
Vol. IIA Discipline	O	O
Vol. IIB-D Programmes	O	O

2 Which parts of the material sent to you before the meeting, did you read?

	thoroughly	superficially	not
Vol. I Countries: Introduction	O	O	O
Country descriptions	O	O	O
Preliminary comparison	O	O	O
Vol. IIA Discipline: Discipline Germany	O	O	O
Programmes Germany	O	O	O
Discipline Netherlands	O	O	O
Programmes Netherlands	O	O	O
Discipline Britain	O	O	O
Programmes Britain	O	O	O
Vol. IIB Germany: course structure	O	O	O
Micro/macro	O	O	O
Quantitative methods	O	O	O
Specialist strands	O	O	O
Vol. IIC Netherlands: course structure	O	O	O
Micro/macro	O	O	O
Quantitative methods	O	O	O
Specialist strands	O	O	O
Vol IID Britain: course structure	O	O	O
Micro/macro	O	O	O
Quantitative methods	O	O	O
Specialist strands	O	O	O

3 Do you think the descriptions are comparable, ie did they help you in comparing the different units with each other:

	yes, or mostly	partly	no, or hardly
Countries (Vol. I)	O	O	O
Discipline-wide features (Vol. II A)	O	O	O
Institutions (Vols. II B, II C, II D)	O	O	O

3a Which countries or cases were described especially good or bad?

. . . .

. . . .

. . . .

. . . .

. . . .

4   Did you make use of the additional material present in Utrecht (Vol. III = 10 blue Volumes)?

yes ⃝   no ⃝

C Peer review meeting in Utrecht

1   Is the purpose of the meeting fulfilled? (reaching statements about the relative strenghts and weaknesses of economics-programmes in order to assess whether graduates from country A are acceptable in country B)

yes ⃝   partly ⃝   no ⃝

2   Is it your opinion that you could have reached the same conlusions about the economics programmes in the three countries without the written documentation?

yes ⃝
no ⃝

3   Is it your opinion that you could have reached the same conlusions about the economics programmes in the three countries with written documentation only?

yes ⃝   no
Go to C.6   Go to C.4

4   If C.2, C.3 = NO. Which alternative way to complement written documentation is, in your opinion, better?

Check one

Site visits to all participating higher education institutions ⃝
One plenary meeting [like this one] ⃝
Several plenary meetings ⃝
Other: . . . . ⃝

5   If C.2, C.3 = NO. Which categories of experts should be present in the visits and/or meeting(s)?

Check one or more

Independent experts from universities etc ⃝
Independent professionals ⃝
Experts from participating institutions à titre personnel ⃝
Experts from participating institutions as representatives ⃝
Other: . . . . ⃝

6 Please rate the importance to you of the various parts of the written material:	thoroughly	superficially	not
Vol. I Countries: Introduction	○	○	○
Country descriptions	○	○	○
Preliminary comparison	○	○	○
Vol. IIA Discipline: Discipline Germany	○	○	○
Programmes Germany	○	○	○
Discipline Netherlands	○	○	○
Programmes Netherlands	○	○	○
Discipline Britain	○	○	○
Programmes Britain	○	○	○
Vol. IIB Germany: course structure	○	○	○
Micro/macro	○	○	○
Quantitative methods	○	○	○
Specialist strands	○	○	○
Vol. IIC Netherlands: course structure	○	○	○
Micro/macro	○	○	○
Quantitative methods	○	○	○
Specialist strands	○	○	○
Vol. IID Britain: course structure	○	○	○
Micro/macro	○	○	○
Quantitative methods	○	○	○
Specialist strands	○	○	○

D Personal data

1 What is your country?

Check one

Germany ○
The Netherlands ○
United Kingdom ○

2 Were you in the 'internal' group (university experts), or in the group of 'external' experts?

internal	extenal
○	○

E Remarks

If you want to make any remarks, please check this Box.   ○

You can make use of the rest of this sheet and the back of it, and add more sheets if necessary.